More Praise for **Philanthropy in a Flat World**

"Don't risk being irrelevant! Like any good fundraising book, Jon reminds us what's important: mission, vision and values; and, donor-centrism and relationship building. But what makes this book so urgently special is Jon's approach: what the globalization of philanthropy means and how it affects the most local and most international organizations. Full of inspiring real-life stories that link to practical strategies, Jon challenges nonprofits and fundraisers to get it together in the flat world. Hurry up, because it's been flat for a while!"

—Simone P. Joyaux, ACFRE
Author of *Keep Your Donors* and
Strategic Fund Development

"Despite his apparent light-hearted portrayal of fundraising theory, Jon has posed some serious questions and—as with all he says—it is worth taking note of his conclusions. After all, there should always be fun in fundraising!"

—Judith Rich, OBE

"The world we live in is smaller today than ever before—but this doesn't mean that it's a simpler place. Jon has examined this phenomenon, confronting the fears and difficulties that we all have as we operate in an increasingly 'flat' world and he's shown us how to grab the opportunities that this new world offers. This is an essential, not an optional read for anyone in the field of philanthropy."

—Andrew Watt, FInstF, Chief Programs Officer
Association of Fundraising Professionals

Philanthropy in
a Flat World

Philanthropy in a Flat World

Inspiration Through Globalization

Jon Duschinsky

WILEY

John Wiley & Sons, Inc.

Published by John Wiley & Sons, Inc., Hoboken, New Jersey.
Published simultaneously in Canada.

For general information on our other products and services, or technical
support, please contact our Customer Care Department within the United
States at 800-762-2974, outside the United States at 317-572-3993 or fax
317-572-4002.

Wiley also publishes its books in a variety of electronic formats. Some content
that appears in print may not be available in electronic books.

For more information about Wiley products, visit our Web site at http://www.
wiley.com.

ISBN: 978-0-470-45801-3

Printed in the United States of America

10 9 8 7 6 5 4 3 2 1

The AFP Fund Development Series

The AFP Fund Development Series is intended to provide fund development professionals and volunteers, including board members (and others interested in the nonprofit sector), with top-quality publications that help advance philanthropy as voluntary action for the public good. Our goal is to provide practical, timely guidance and information on fundraising, charitable giving, and related subjects. The Association of Fundraising Professionals (AFP) and Wiley each bring to this innovative collaboration unique and important resources that result in a whole greater than the sum of its parts. For information on other books in the series, please visit:

www.afpnet.org

The Association of Fundraising Professionals

The Association of Fundraising Professionals (AFP) represents over 30,000 members in more than 197 chapters throughout the United States, Canada, Mexico, and China, working to advance philanthropy through advocacy, research, education, and certification programs.

The association fosters development and growth of fundraising professionals and promotes high ethical standards in the fundraising profession. For more information or to join the world's largest association of fundraising professionals, visit www.afpnet.org.

2008–2009 AFP Publishing Advisory Committee

Chair: **Nina P. Berkheiser, CFRE**
Principal Consultant, Your Nonprofit Advisor

Linda L. Chew, CFRE
Development Consultant

D. C. Dreger, ACFRE
Senior Campaign Director, Custom Development Solutions, Inc. (CDS)

Patricia L. Eldred, CFRE
Director of Development, Independent Living Inc.

Samuel N. Gough, CFRE
Principal, The AFRAM Group

Audrey P. Kintzi , ACFRE
Director of Development, Courage Center

Steven Miller, CFRE
Director of Development and Membership, Bread for the World

Robert J. Mueller, CFRE
Vice President, Hospice Foundation of Louisville

Maria Elena Noriega
Director, Noriega Malo & Associates

Michele Pearce
Director of Development, Consumer Credit Counseling
Service of Greater Atlanta

Leslie E. Weir, MA, ACFRE
Director of Family Philanthropy, The Winnipeg
Foundation

Sharon R. Will, CFRE
Director of Development, South Wind Hospice

John Wiley & Sons, Inc.:

Susan McDermott
Senior Editor (Professional/Trade Division)

AFP Staff:

Jan Alfieri
Manager, New Product Development

Rhonda Starr
Vice President, Education and Training

Contents

Contents

Philanthropy in
a Flat World

Introduction

The First Flat World Fundraiser

It was a hot Saturday in August. A day to be etched forever in the minds of millions. The day that a black pastor from Atlanta, Georgia, stood before 250,000 people on the National Mall in the capital city of the United States. The day that a moment of history was recorded. The day of "I have a dream." And the day that fundraising entered the flat world.

Martin Luther King Jr. was 34 years old when he uttered those words. Born in 1929 to a father who was a preacher and a mother who was a church organist, he was thrust, somewhat against his will, into the spotlight in the aftermath of Rosa Parks' historic refusal to give up her bus seat to a white person.

He was a figurehead of the Civil Rights movement, a key player in the political and social change of the early 1960s in the United States and ultimately across the world. But what is more important for us, he was arguably the first Flat World Fundraiser.

On that August day in Washington, King had prepared his speech—typed as usual on a portable type-writer. Indeed, he was making changes to it until the final moments before stepping onto the stage. But when he stood in front of the tumultuous crowd—the size of which had never before been seen in Washington—he stopped, ditched his papers, and moved back to a speech he had given a few months previously. Why? Nerves (a quarter of a million people are a lot of eyes staring back at you), or did the universe simply speak to him? We will never know.

What we do know is that Martin Luther King had "had a dream" before, in Detroit and Chicago, to name but two occasions. Yet his epiphany came that hot day in Washington. What was different? The answer is simple— television. His address on Washington Mall, in the shadow of Abraham Lincoln, was covered live by all three major TV networks of the time. This was a gargantuan event.

Introduction

And it transformed his message into the battle cry of a generation of both black and white men and women who dreamed, like him, of a fairer society in the United States.

The media and the message came together in a way such that "the right word, emotionally charged, reach[ed] the whole person and change[d] the relationships of men" (Stephen Oates).

Martin Luther King was a messenger. He was a communicator, and he was a builder of relationships between people—millions of them, all around the United States. He was, in its purest sense, a fundraiser, bringing together people through a shared vision in a call to action. And he led the message into the homes of millions. It was a simple message—a pure message, easy to remember and easy to appropriate. From this message came action.

Without the flat world—a world of instant information transfer, of sharing, of media power and concentration—Dr. King's message that day in Washington would have had only as much impact as when he had delivered it previously in Detroit or Chicago. The flat world allowed his message to flow freely from one individual to another across the planet in the blink of an eye. It allowed him to instill the courage and the energy in millions of people to continue the fight for their rights. And it allowed him to inspire fundraisers and other visionaries around the world to bring about more change, different change, much-needed change. The flat world was Martin Luther King's platform, and without knowing it, he had opened the way for hundreds, thousands, even millions of individuals to be the change they want to see in the world.

Welcome to tomorrow.

Part One

FLAT AND BEAUTIFUL

Chapter One

The Flat World

From Columbus to Skinny Lattes

Before Christopher Columbus, Vasco da Gama, and others took up the challenge of the unknown and sailed out into the wide oceans to look for and conquer new lands, we believed the world was flat. We could see until a certain point, and then the land and ocean started to disappear.

Then our explorer friends, helped, incidentally, by Galileo and astronomers everywhere, allowed us to realize that actually our planet was round. It was spinning through a universe of other stars and planets, all of which seemed to be round, too. The round world was characterized by distance, by different cultures, by uncharted territories. . . .

And then, in the latter part of the twentieth century, the world got flat again. Everything that had defined the round world was suddenly brought into question. You could fly from one side of the world to another in less than a day without ever moving from seat 24B. You could hold a conversation with another person of a totally different culture in a different time zone, in a shared language, at any time of the day or night. And that was before the Internet. Now, the world is literally at your fingertips, and Google is working toward becoming the ultimate Big Brother and trying to put at our fingertips all the information that has ever existed in the world.

As we shall see later, the flat world is an incredible playing field for us all. It has brought opportunity to bring change in a way that we could never have dreamed about just 20 years ago. It has put us in a world of incredible wealth and at the same time given us the keys to solve poverty. It has altered perceptions and interactions in a nonreversible and very positive way, by giving information to those who never had it before. But it has also brought something that we need to be acutely aware of—responsibility. With opportunity comes responsibility. With responsibility comes the role of the individual: you and me; them and us.

And it has come NOW.

So what is the flat world? Where did it come from, and why am I writing a book about it?

Thomas Friedman, the *New York Times* columnist, wrote a book in 2005 that has become a reference point in flat world thinking. *The World Is Flat* (Farrar, Straus & Giroux) has not only become a global best seller, but it has challenged a number of taboos on the subject, setting the basis for further thinking and development (of which this book is unashamedly a part). Together, we will be calling on some of Friedman's work to better understand the concepts at play in the flat world, but our focus here will be on how these trends are, and will be, impacting on fundraising and the development of philanthropy around the world.

As we set out on this journey, may I humbly make a suggestion? Suspend your preconceptions. And remember how much the world has changed in the past few years. Just 10 years ago, how many of us had an iPhone, an iPod, or a lightweight notebook computer? How many of us complained because of the number of e-mails we received? Who had a Facebook page or stopped on their way to work to pick up a skinny latte while checking their multiple e-mail accounts on their BlackBerrys? Who still uses a fax machine? The world has become exponential and shows no sign at all of slowing down. So let's start from the hypothesis that everything we think we know about tomorrow is very, very likely to be wrong . . . and then we shouldn't be too far from the truth.

Flat, Wild, and Wacky

The flat world is the result of globalization—of people coming together to share, collaborate, and interact in a way that has never happened before. A few months ago Wikipedia had this to say of globalization: "It refers to increasing global connectivity, integration and interdependence in the economic, social, technological, cultural, political and ecological spheres." This definition is, by itself, meaningless. Wikis are one of the products of the flat world—totally open, interactive platforms that allow any reader to become a contributor, changing content and then publishing it for all to see. Wikipedia is of course the best-known, and builds on the collaborative expertise of millions of people around the world to create what has become since its creation the world's biggest dictionary and encyclopedia. It is a pure product of globalization, something that would have been unthinkable just 10 years ago. However, it has one fault. It is a normalizer. The instant collaboration brings with it the ability to define concepts and words in the most complete way possible. But in the process, the senses of the concepts become distorted. And concepts as difficult as "globalization" become totally incoherent. We see connectivity, interdependence, and integration—words that show how the global playing field is becoming increasingly a web of interaction. But to be honest, this doesn't help much.

David Rothkopf was an advisor to the Clinton administration and a key thinker around the concepts of globalization. This is what he has to say: "Globalization is the word we came up with to describe the changing relationships between governments and big business. But what is going on today is a much broader, much more profound phenomenon. It is about things that impact some of the deepest, most ingrained aspects of society. This is not just about organizations and businesses interacting; it is about the emergence of totally new social, political, and business models."

What is certain is that globalization is a phenomenon that is the confluence of a number of key processes and subprocesses that are impacting all around our society. Globalization is nowhere and everywhere at the same time. It is intangible and yet very, very tangible. It is. Period.

It has fans, and it has detractors. It has people who meet at G-8 summits to shout their anger, while it has people who meet in Beverly Hills salons to flaunt their dollars. It brings us together, and it divides us. Again, it is. Period.

And this is one of the biggest problems with globalization. It is. And no one is responsible. There is no one individual or company or government that we can pin the responsibility for globalization on. Even Bill Gates, widely seen as being the closest we can get to a human incarnation of globalization, cannot be held entirely responsible. And this is exactly why people get so angry about it. We are cause-and-effect animals.

The Flat World

Events in our society typically have a cause, and if they don't we try our hardest to find one (think attorneys). But because no one is entirely responsible for globalization, because no government, no individual, no company is directly the cause, we are faced with a problem. We have no one to blame! We have no one to turn on to vent our spleen, to whine to about stuff we can't control and that scares us, to challenge and shout at because things are happening that we don't understand. We don't know who to blame for financial crises—governments, banks, or greedy businesses? All of the above? Quite simply, we are stuck.

And then it gets worse. Because when we realise that globalization and the ills of the world are not the fault of one person, one group, one party, or one nation in particular, that nobody is truly responsible, we have a show-stopping "aha" moment. Because if nobody is responsible, then in some way we are all responsible. And that is the problem. Because, fundamentally, we are *not* very responsible.

We are consumers who yearn for lower prices and who want to eat avocados all year at rock-bottom prices even if they have to be flown halfway around the world. But we (or our friends and families) are workers in industries where our jobs are at risk. We are human beings who thrive in the luxury of our SUVs, but we are parents who are scared sick about the state of the planet we are leaving for our children.

We are, as humans, famous for our paradoxes. But globalization has made the whole thing starker—we know we should take the train and reduce our carbon footprint, but it's still so tempting to jump in the car, crank up the air-conditioning, plug in the iPod, and create a little travel haven of individualism. If globalization is one thing, it is the freeing up of hundreds of individual factors and processes to follow their natural tendency to move toward efficiency at all costs. And it is. Period.

It is the trigger and the symptom at the same time, the underlying cause and the realization. And it is leading us into a world where the unlikely and the improbable are becoming probable. Where the extremes are leading the middle. Where, as Jonas Ridderstrale and Kjell Nordstrom point out in their fantastic book *Karaoke Capitalism*

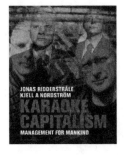

(Praeger, 2005), "the best rapper in the US is white. Where the best golfer is black. Where France accuses the US of arrogance in its diplomacy."

The world has been turned upside down: if you were to visit the International Fundraising Congress in the Netherlands each October, you would find yourself among people from over 60 countries and, as happened to me a couple of years ago, you might find yourself having breakfast with a person from Nepal who is using common sense and a bit of creativity to raise money from rich Nepalese for projects to help poor Nepalese. Or maybe you could just simply check out the financial flows of Western Union, and look at how much money from rich Indian families in Delhi and Bangalore is now flowing into poor, depressed Indian communities in the United Kingdom. Or how much money from successful Mexican entrepreneurs is now flowing into deprived Mexican communities in the United States.

We live in a world where foundations and non-governmental organizations (NGOs) are multinationals, where multinationals are foundations, and where the divide between haves and have-nots, between rich and poor, is no longer geographic. We live in a world where the infant mortality rate in Washington, D.C., is the same as in Sri Lanka. We live in a world where the biggest and most successful NGO in the Ukraine is a mail-order company. We live in a world where each person in Western Europe will be on the receiving end of up to 1,800 communications, including branding and advertising messages, each day.

We live in a wild, wacky, slightly confusing, and terribly fast-moving world.

From Geography to Biography

So, how did we get here?

Thomas Friedman argues that globalization as we know it today actually has its origins back in 1492 and has gone through three major stages of evolution since then. This is, perhaps, a slightly U.S.-centric model, but one that does have a certain logic.

The first phase of globalization started with Columbus. Whether or not he did actually discover anything, he is credited with bridging the divide between the *old world* of Europe and the *new world* of North and South

America. This period (from the fifteenth century to the late eighteenth century) was one of terrible tumult in Europe, with wars, revolutions, and just simple bickering among ruling classes taking up much of the continent's energy and resources. It was also the period of the founding of the new world, with the first settlers arriving in what would become the United States and Canada to forge new communities and in doing so committing genocides from which the North American psyche has never quite recovered. It was the opening up of travel and trade between continents, a time in history when countries and muscles mattered more than anything else. If you wanted to play with the big boys, you had to show how much brute force (horsepower, wind power, steam power) your country had and how creatively it could deploy it (mostly through wars and other such uses of man's talent). It was a time of national globalization—of imperialism, of empires—of countries going global for the first time.

The second phase of globalization came with the industrial revolution and ended with the digital revolution, and was a period of unprecedented growth and wealth creation. Friedman argues that this was when the world went from "size medium to size small." What powered this growth was no longer national imperialism, but corporate imperialism—companies, from the textile mills of nineteenth-century northern England to the multinationals that dominate our choices and supermarket shelves today—taking control of capital and opportunity and going global to search for new markets for their products and cheaper labor sources for their production.

And what fueled this power was a combination of falling transportation costs (from horse to ship to railway to airplane), and falling telecommunication costs (from telegraph to telephone to satellite and fiber optics).

So from *countries* with global ambition, we moved to *companies* with global ambition. And then globalization as we know it hit, and we moved to *individuals* with global ambition.

I wonder if you are one of the very few people in the world who used airline transport more pre-2000 than you are doing now. (I did the calculation recently and wondered if I shouldn't start buying shares in a carbon offsetting company.) Or think about how you communicated pre-Y2K. Mobile phones? E-mail? Internet? How did we ever live without them?

The past seven years have seen exponential change, on a scale never before witnessed by humanity. The world has gone, in one fell swoop, from "size small to a size tiny." We are communicating, travelling, collaborating, exchanging information, thinking, and working together with people all over the world in a completely new way. In a way that has never been seen before. In a way that was completely and totally unimaginable (except to a select few) just a few years ago. This is the world of tomorrow. And it is going at Mach 3.

But this wild, flat world has brought with it another change, equally fundamental and equally unexpected. It has created the individual revolution: the third phase of globalization.

Today with a PC and a link to the Internet, you are a global company. You can reach every other individual or organization that also has a PC and a link to the Internet. It is the widest, most incredibly powerful market that has ever existed. If you are a fundraiser and you have a link to the Internet, you are potentially an international NGO.

Individuals are now in a position where they can make a difference through virtual networks of like-minded individuals around the world. Geography has been replaced by biography. And these individuals are creating organizations. They are enabling, empowering, and collaborating globally through the flat world.

The individual has taken back the earth—and (thankfully) not just white middle-class individuals from Western, developed economies. Chinese, Indians, Africans, Russians, Hungarians . . . large and small, young and old, rich and poor are taking part.

Globalization has led us to the flat world—a world where college students from India can start up a small company doing subcontracted game design for French software houses and less than 10 years later purchase the rights for Charlie Chaplin's image.

It is a world where Benyam Addis, an Ethiopian student at a recent class of mine, can come to the United States and study philanthropy and fundraising in order to develop his nonprofit organization helping children back in Ethiopia. A world where individuals have the tools and the opportunity to make changes in a way they never had before. A world where the words of Martin Luther King have never rung so true.

There is perhaps one other way of putting this transition. We went from a pre-industrial age, where the majority of activity was subsistence farming, to an industrial age, where steam power, machine tools, and electricity brought incredible new wealth, to the information age, where computers and the Internet have enabled people to link together and become much more productive.

But we have now moved even out of the information age. We have entered a new era: one of new challenges, and one where the power might actually really go to the people. It is not the *digital age,* as many would have us believe. We have entered the *talent age.*

In the talent age, the information tools developed during the information age have become a commodity: cheap and easily available, if not free. Think open source. I recently heard a radio interview on French public radio with a member of the open source community who claimed that open source companies now employ over 25,000 people in France alone—by making products that are free! The source code that used to be the most guarded secret of software companies—the crown jewels of their economic success—is now being given away.

The tools or the products that do things, or allow us to do things—in this case to access and interpret information—are no longer what makes the money. It is the service that goes with them, that supports them, and that drives them. Of course, this has been the case in other industries for many years. Carmakers have long since made more money from financing than from the cars themselves, and radio and television media have always been free at point of sale. But the open source model is the first time that this notion of free has been run out to the whole business model. Media need advertising. Open source companies only need you to want to engage with their free product in such a way that you enjoy it, find it useful, and want to engage with it further.

During much of the production of this book, I used an online tool called YouSendIt (www.yousendit.com) that allows you to transfer large files for free over the Web. No more hassles with e-mails that get lost or bounce because they contain files that are too weighty for Outlook or Entourage. Simply upload the file, put in your e-mail address and the address of the recipient of the file, and send it off. At one point, I found myself reading through an e-mail from the company asking me whether I wanted to upgrade to a subscription version, thereby parting me from my cash, to get faster upload times. Having engaged with the product and enjoyed it, and having recommended it to friends, I felt that I was ready to take that step. I had been successfully open sourced! The product itself was a commodity, with limited value. But the value could be created by adding to the product—making it faster, sexier, easier to use, and so on—and all at a price.

In today's commodity world, competitive advantage is no longer about having more. It is no longer about quantity. It is about quality, niches, and relationships. It is about understanding the entry point for a relationship—in this case, giving me a useful product for free that I was so impressed with that I raved about it to anyone who would listen—and then working from there with talent and imagination. It is about being different, making yourself stand out from the crowd, and being the Purple Cow that Seth Godin introduced us to a few years ago in his book of the same name.

And all this requires a *huge* sea change in the way we position, develop, and market our products—or in the case of the philanthropic sector, our causes. Because quite simply it is no longer about the product or the cause. If I feel strongly about saving whales, I have a choice of probably a dozen organizations in any given Western European or North American country that would happily help me part with my money to save a humpback or two. So what is going to influence my choice? Obviously brand awareness is one factor, and a pretty important one indeed. So is the fact that the charity actually asks me for money. But what about the experience I have as a donor? Increasingly we know that the donor experience is key, especially to repeat giving. And I would argue that donor experience is now *the* key. In a world where quantity has been replaced by quality, loyalty and repeat giving are the only ways to survive. There is no point in spending hundreds of thousands of dollars on recruiting a database full of donors if they each make only one donation. And crunch time happens when people start transferring their giving, not only from one organization to another, but from one cause to another, according to donor experience.

But hang on a minute . . . this definition of crunch time sounds remarkably like what has already been happening for a number of years. Don't donors make informed giving decisions according to how they feel about an organization? Not a cause, but an organization? When, in 1995, the CEO of the French cancer charity, the Association for Cancer Research (ARC), was arrested for embezzlement, huge numbers of their donors did not just move their giving away from the charity, they moved it away from the cause. If ARC was their favorite charity, they moved their giving to their second favorite charity, which most likely meant a different cause. Ask a group of people how many of their top five nonprofits are all for the same cause. How many do you think give to five different cancer organizations, or five different anti-drunk-driving causes?

So let's take a step back, here. What we are saying is that the box is now more important than what is inside it. That the after-sales (or after-donation) service is more important than the donation or the product itself. And that we need to move our thinking to embracing and accepting this ASAP.

It needs us all to not just think outside the box (indeed, recently a friend of mine remarked that these days there are so many people thinking outside the box that it has become cool to think inside it), but to fundamentally shift our thinking. And as so often has happened in the past few years, those Californian design and psychology geniuses at Apple were ahead of the game on this one. "Think different" was a downright revolutionary slogan back in the 1980s when Apple first used it in its advertising. (See Exhibit 1.1.)

Exhibit 1.1   Apple Advertisement

The Flat World

Truly "thinking different" requires huge effort and commitment. It requires risk, energy, and talent—lots and lots of talent. Because talent allows us to take the product, the cause or the traditional way of looking at something, and turn it on its head. The industrial and information ages were about learning how to be the norm, learning how to be productive, to be stable, to be middle of the road. Learning how to be a good team player who got promotions and moved up the ladder with the cause you cared about most. Learning how to be a company that had stable clients and innovated slowly so as not to scare them off. Learning how to watch what your competitors were doing and copy it as soon as you could to be sure to gain valuable points of market share.

But today, we need to unlearn that. We need to deprogram ourselves. We need to deprogram our children, our education system, our universities, our organizations. We need to stop trying to be someone else, and start working out what it is that makes us *us*. We need to work out who we are, and who we want to be. And once we've figured it out, we need to shout it loud and proud from all of the rooftops. We need to not just Think Different, but Act Different, Behave Different, Dream Different, and Change Different.

In our oversupplied world of individualism and choice (both of which by-products of globalization we will go into more later), whatever it is that we do has become a commodity. Our new product has already gone out of date by the time we put it to market. Our new concept will have been copied within 30 seconds if it looks like it might work.

Zoom

If you live today in a major metropolitan center in large areas of the global North, there is a fair chance that you have either seen, spoken to, been accosted by, enjoyed the presence of, or just downright ignored a face-to-face (F2F) fundraiser. It was, in much of Western Europe, the "next big thing" in charity development in the late 1990s and early part of this century. The concept is terribly simple—young, energetic, and passionate people stand on the streets of big cities and try to start conversations with passers-by that, it is hoped, will lead to the folks on the street being so convinced that they sign up immediately to become regular monthly donors to the charity through standing order or funds transfer. Face-to-face fundraising first saw the light of day in Vienna, in 1996, in the offices of Greenpeace. Daryl Upsall worked at Greenpeace International headquarters at the time and recalls how it came about:

"In 1993, we sent George Smith and Ken Burnett, two of the profession's most recognized experts, out around the world to look at fundraising. We knew we had a challenge. Greenpeace had become Graypeace—our average donor age was over 55, our global income was in decline, and we needed to do something radical. At the time, 18 percent of our income was coming through regular monthly giving, and the idea we had was to move the whole organization into monthly direct debit around the world. But we needed a tool to do it. The answer came from Austria, of all places, in June 1995. Jasna Sonne from Greenpeace Austria and a local company called Dialog Direct were having lunch at a restaurant in Vienna, and they had the idea that it would be great to go and recruit a thousand people in the streets of Vienna to do a monthly direct debit via a special bank form. Everyone thought it was crazy. But we tested it. It was so successful within a small period of time that the Austrian church called a debate in the parliament to complain that Greenpeace was being so successful in recruiting donors that it was stealing the money that should be going into collection boxes on Sundays in church."

By the time Daryl Upsall left Greenpeace in 2001, monthly giving had risen to 58 percent of all income, and is now up to 70 percent, giving the charity a huge advantage in challenging economic times.

A great idea that came out of a lunch meeting in Austria is now raising money for charities across the world, from Chile to China. Indeed, the best results and growth are coming from places like Thailand, India, and South Korea! As Daryl says, "the fact that a fundraising tool from Austria could become a hit in South Korea still blows my mind!"

Ideas move incredibly fast in the flat philanthropic world. Conferences, the Internet, articles in newspapers and magazines that then get blogged and sent around the world. . . . Information is no longer power. Today, power is the ability to transform that information into something that differentiates your organization and your cause. Something that attracts people to your brand, that makes them sit up and think, "Yes, I want to help *your* organization, rather than the 500 others around the world that appear do the same thing." We cannot please all of the people all of the time. And we should stop trying to. With a bit of luck, we can use new ideas and new technology to help us please a small niche of people most of the time—just like Greenpeace does. Done well, that is enough to live, thrive, and survive in the flat philanthropic world.

What Makes a Pancake?

We cannot really understand where we are and work out where we are going if we do not have a clearer idea of how we got here. Thomas Friedman identifies 10 processes, or flatteners, that have played an important, if not essential, role in moving us toward this globalized society. I have taken these 10 flatteners and put them in a philanthropic context. What emerges are four major trends: political, technological, human, and economic.

Political Trends

Politics has played a huge part in our lives as citizens of the world in the past 100 years. From the two world wars to the cold war, politics, politicians, and political ideologies have been a staple in twentieth-century life. But the absolute reign of politics arguably came to an end on November 9, 1989, the day the Berlin Wall fell.

My father was born in London in the late 1940s to a German mother and a Czech father, both of whom were Jewish refugees who had managed to escape before doing so became impossible. They both lost most of their families to the concentration camps and tried to rebuild a new life for themselves in England. My father had been to Germany during the 1960s, had stood by the Brandenburg Gate and Checkpoint Charlie in Berlin, and had looked over to the East German part of the city—to that world that seemed forever cut off and distant.

For him and his parents (my grandparents), the fall of the Berlin Wall was an electroshock. I remember waking up one morning around that time, perhaps even the day following the tearing down of the wall, to find my father's ear glued to the radio, to the news, to the incredible opening up of the world, to the overwhelming events that were happening. I had rarely seen him so moved.

For Europeans, all over the continent, the fall of the Berlin Wall was life-changing. Imagine a bottle of champagne that has been shaken consistently for 50 years, but the cork has been held in place. Imagine suddenly releasing the cork.

For people on the other side, who had lived with oppression and distrust for decades, the effect was electrifying.

Balazs Sator is a fundraiser and trainer who lives today in Hungary. Recognized today as one of the leading lights in the Eastern and Central European nonprofit world, he is particularly well placed to tell this experience firsthand.

"I grew up in a small village about 50 kilometers outside of Bratislava in what is now called Slovakia, but back then was part of Czechoslovakia. What was brutal during Soviet times was that growing up it became clear that unless the situation changed, or I became a party member, I was never going to get the chance to go to the West. You can see Vienna from one of the hills in Bratislava and yet it was forbidden territory. I was too young to say it felt horrible, but that border was so much in the middle of my life.

"Not everyone was a revolutionary—we started understanding some of these things as a generation because everyone recognized that something was wrong, that the system was wrong. This was 1988 and the beginning of the period of change. There was a huge force at that time—I still have goose bumps now when I think of what happened. My village was outside Bratislava, and we traveled in every day for the demonstrations. Despite the police brutality, we still went out on the street day in and day out because we had realized that if we weren't there then we would be guilty of not being a part of the change. Crime fell by almost 70 percent. People started to think differently. It began with the blue ribbons—people who supported the revolution started pinning blue ribbons on their jackets. Some who were not brave enough wore them inside their clothes. Then people started lighting candles in their windows.

The Flat World

"It was December 1989, after the fall of the Berlin Wall, that I finally got the chance to travel over the border to Austria. I waited on a bus for nine hours in Bratislava to travel to Vienna. We didn't believe that our passports would be accepted! As we stepped out of the bus in Vienna, suddenly the joy of actually being there was turned into shock at the incredible difference between the two countries—what people were buying there, the shops they had, the cafés they were sitting in. For us, Czechoslovaks, it was unbelievable.

"Even if the euphoria around the revolution quickly turned to the challenges of building a democracy, it doesn't take anything away from the fact that this change was produced by hundreds of thousands of individuals coming together. And even if I was just one of them, I am proud today to have been there. Finally I can do as I wish and I can achieve what I am capable of. Something changed in the environment, and you can be the cork that pops out of the bottle. For me this was the biggest value of the changes—individual responsibility and rights *do* matter, and that is what has taken me to fundraising. Individuals fundraising for a better world represent one of the forces behind democracy."

As Balazs so poignantly illustrates, the opening of the Soviet bloc was a clear victory for the capitalist model, one based on individual enterprise and multinational collaboration, which was now recognized openly across the world as being the predominant model of growth. But it was also a clear victory of the individual over the body politic—of the vision of individuals, forming themselves into virtual coalitions and organizations of like-minded souls and overcoming a government armed both with machine guns and with ideology. The individual had, through association, brought about change—huge change that would impact on lives around the world for decades to come. Not even 20 years on from this victory of the individual and civil society, there are now over 250,000 active nonprofit organizations in Russia. Most of these are involved at some level with philanthropy, and a Carnegie Report in 2003 showed that some 85 percent of Russian companies had corporate social or philanthropic activities. Eighty five percent of Russian companies!

Technological Trends

Technology has arguably been the most vital catalyst in creating the flat world. It has allowed each and every one of us, thanks to mobile phones and wireless technology, to work anywhere and to be in contact with the rest of the world 24/7. This chapter is being written from the deck of a friend's house in San Jose, California, but this morning I checked back with the office in Paris, France, e-mailed partners in South America and the UK, and participated in a teleconference with a client in Canada. At the end of the day, challenge yourself to think about how long it might have taken you to achieve everything that you have done in one day without your PC, the Internet, software, and telecommunications.

And if the exponential growth in computing power carries on as predicted, it is estimated that this side of 2050 a home PC will be able to carry out more calculations per second than the combined brains of every human on the planet! And it will, of course, be able to feed the information generated by these calculations to you wherever you are, by wireless and satellite technology. These are startling predictions—terrifying, even. But we don't have to look so far into the future—it is estimated that by 2010, the amount of information in the world will be doubling every 72 hours. Let's just mull that over for a moment: Every three days, the total amount of information on the planet will be doubling.

This has huge implications for the world we live in. It means that if you are a nonprofit organization, by the time you are finishing your next three-year strategic plan, you could be, in theory, talking to a completely different audience of potential supporters—with individuals able to access more information on your cause, your organization, your performance, and your competitors than ever before, more easily than ever before, and more quickly than ever before. They will have more information, more knowledge, more options, more choices. They will be exponentially more powerful. Think Facebook— and think how long many organizations took to understand it. It may be that the next trend that impacts us will be over before we can actually capitalize on it if we don't smarten up to the way technology is moving everything faster than ever before.

Human Trends

Technology now allows us to do things we could not even have dreamt about 10 years ago. Technorati's

The Flat World

State of the Blogosphere 2008 study cites figures from Universal McCann claiming that 184 million people have started a blog worldwide and that 364 million Web users worldwide are now blog readers.

That is almost 200 million people who have decided to share their thoughts, their work or their lives with anyone who simply cares to click and read. And almost double that number seek out information through blogs. The whole system has empowered the individual to take the act of communicating information into his or her own hands. You don't like what you are hearing on CNN or the BBC? Well then, pick up your mobile phone, and go and stand outside a TV studio ready to ask questions of the politicians as they leave. Record their interviews, snap a couple of photos, write the whole thing up giving it your particular angle, and suddenly you don't need cable news anymore. Indeed, independent journalism is now a huge business, and thousands of individuals across the world who are dissatisfied with the quality of reporting offered by traditional media are starting their own news blogs. Today, in the era of technology multitasking, with a simple phone that has a camera and an MP3 recorder, anyone can communicate information.

Please note that this doesn't mean that anyone can be a journalist, and (while this is not the place for a rant) I do feel strongly that, as a society, we are losing the value of real investigative journalism and thus endangering the subtle balance of democracy by removing many of the fail-safe mechanisms that great journalism provides.

As we discuss the human trends, let's return for a moment to open source. Perhaps one of the most remarkable and unexpected human developments to come out of technology, open source is truly revolutionizing many sectors of the economy. The idea of individuals working together collaboratively online to develop, improve, and share software and hardware has fundamentally changed the business models of many leading-edge companies. While in Silicon Valley writing and researching this book, I began to understand the power of the human being, through technology, to develop the tools that will allow other human beings to express themselves and work better, faster, and more intelligently.

Open source, and the doors it opens (such as peer-to-peer sharing of content, music, video, etc.), will continue to impact on the world we live in, moving slowly, sector by sector, like a creeping giant. The nonprofit world and how it funds itself will inevitably be impacted. And we have the opportunity today to anticipate rather than be a victim of that change. Let's not fall into the same trap as major record companies, for example, which instead of trying to embrace changes in technology and search for new and profitable business models during the 1990s and early 2000s, spent their time sticking their heads in the sand and fighting the inevitable, with catastrophic results for their bottom lines.

Offering donors new ways to create their interactions with nonprofits, using new technology to collaborate with donors and beneficiaries in order to meet their needs in a more effective and efficient way, opening up our (often slightly stuffy and opaque) organizations for all to see— these will all be on the agenda for tomorrow's fundraising team meetings. We have a choice. Pretend it's not there and suffer the consequences, or anticipate and make the most of what is an incredible opportunity to help further our missions.

In the flat philanthropic world, one elected official alone cannot solve the problems of eight million people, but eight million people networked together can solve a city's problems. Think YouTube. Think Barack Obama.

A word of warning, though, when going down this path: you must do it in a way that truly empowers, not just directs people's energy toward your cause. The individual is king in the new flat world, and if individuals feel that they are not being trusted and empowered, the relationship could be short-lived. The 2007 election campaign in France is a fantastic example of what happens when we try to put too much order and focus into open sourcing.

The candidate for the French left, or labor party, Ségolène Royale, made headlines around the world with her "participative democracy" approach—with its foundations in the open-source Web. The campaign created a number of web sites and blogs (the "Ségosphère"), which were designed to give French people an opportunity to participate in an exercise in online democracy, raising and discussing issues through the Web in a format that was intended to empower in a very positive way. The Web campaign was hugely successful, but failed to bring together the necessary majority to elect the candidate. Why? Aside from the fact that the woman in question was probably unelectable, many commentators claimed that the Web tool was used as a gadget, not really networking people, but just giving them a platform to vent their everyday, run-of-the-mill qualms and complaints. This created the expectation that if the candidate were elected, the issues would be dealt with. And in the end, the candidate herself was simply not able to retain the necessary credibility to follow through on her own new open source system.

This expectations trap, where our capacity to raise an issue does not match our ability to do something about it, was incredibly deftly avoided by Barack Obama's presidential campaign. It is almost as if the Americans learned from the French mistakes! Obama and his team brought together a virtual network of over two million people in one of the most astutely crafted pieces of online mobilization ever seen. Where Ségolène Royale talked about the problems and encouraged people to share their gripes in the hope that they would become part of the bigger picture, Obama centered his campaign around two words—*hope* and *change*—two of the vaguest words in the English language, but words that evoke passion and emotion. It is strange to think that semantics could have been an integral part of a political campaign, but Obama's decision to *not* position the online movement around tangibles, but around intangibles, shows just how clever the Democrats can be when they put their minds to it.

Barack Obama has taken the open source concept to a whole new place, one that we, as nonprofits or agents of change, can learn from and adopt.

Economic Factors

A few years ago, I was lucky enough to visit China and spend three weeks with my partner traveling around the country, from south to north and east to west— from Tibet to Hong Kong via Xian and finally finishing up in Beijing. To say it was memorable would be an understatement. But one particular memory from the trip has remained stuck in the front of mind ever since. It happened in Beijing, an incredible and confusing city. After having been in town for a day or so, we left our hotel as usual in one of Beijing's many suburbs to head into the center and continue our discovery of China's capital. After a visit to the Forbidden City in excruciating heat, made bearable only by the fact that the English commentary in the audio guide was provided by Roger Moore (somewhat of a coup for British intelligence, I thought at the time!), we returned to our hotel—or at least where we thought our hotel was. Everything around where the hotel should have been looked incredibly unfamiliar. There were cranes and building sites where there shouldn't have been. There were no buildings where there should have been, or at least where there had been that very morning. We eventually found our hotel, still standing. But a whole block opposite had been simply flattened in the course of a single day. Who knows where the people who were living that morning in the houses opposite slept that evening? When we left three days later, the first concrete pillars of a new tower block construction were already poking out of the ground.

And then it dawned on me. This was China. Not China of today, but China of tomorrow—a country where whole blocks are flattened in one fell swoop in just a few hours. Where the central planning machine—whose one ambition is growth at all costs—is bulldozing everything in its way.

The economic opening of China and India is such a part of our everyday lives that we tend to forget that it has happened only in the past 10 to 15 years. Bangalore is fast becoming home to most of the back offices of European, North American, and Japanese companies. As Dinakar Singh, a Wall Street hedge fund manager, remarks in *The World Is Flat,* "India had no resources and no infrastructure. It produced people with quality and by quantity. But many of them rotted on the docks of India like vegetables. Only a relative few could get on ships and get out. Not anymore, because we built this ocean crosser, called fiberoptic cable. . . . For decades you had to leave India to be a professional. . . . Now you can plug into the world from India."

The Global Passport for Change

Outsourcing and offshoring are two very integral parts of business models across the world. Any service, call center, business support operation, or knowledge work that can be digitized can now be sourced globally to the cheapest, smartest, and most efficient provider—wherever they happen to be.

My team and I recently worked on a Web project for a charity in France. The client wanted to work with an international team but didn't know where to start, so we built a group of consultants and agencies who collaborated, horizontally, on producing value for the client. Where were they geographically based? In Argentina, Canada, the United States, the United Kingdom, and France. Did they ever meet? No. All collaboration was done by e-mail, coordinated from our office in Paris. The strategy was done by one part of the team, the design and build by another. Everybody contributed new ideas and thinking, including best practices and experiences from each team member's country. Was the charity happy? You bet!

The flat world allows us all, wherever we are, to access the best people on the planet. We are no longer limited to working with the people or organizations in our towns, or in our regions, or even in our countries. As long as the content in question can be digitized, you now have a global passport for change and the freedom to work with whom you want, when you want, regardless of time zones.

Outsourcing (taking parts of the organization and subcontracting their activity) and offshoring (moving whole activities, often in manufacturing, overseas for cheaper labor costs) are currently producing some very vehement discussions in Europe and North America. Chinese textiles and Indian call centers are very much seen to be the bad boys of globalization—taking our jobs, preventing us from ensuring financial security for our children, and in the case of the call centers causing us hours of frustration. Although I don't want to get too much into a debate that would merit another book to discuss fully, I think it is important as agents of change and developers of philanthropy to address this question, if only briefly, as we are likely to see the impact of these global trends on giving in the near future.

The idea is that anything that we can make or outsource more cheaply in other areas of the world will be made or outsourced there. This means huge challenges for Western societies and loads of job losses.

The Flat World

But I think that the real issue here is not jobs, but the polarization of capital. When a U.S. company takes part of its manufacturing to China in order to decrease costs, stay competitive, and ultimately increase profits, the people making money out of the process are the company and its shareholders—not those who are on the lower rungs of the job ladder. While the Chinese workers benefit from increased employment opportunities, the profit is ultimately taken out of China and benefits rich Americans. The capital becomes increasingly polarized, and goes to those individuals with the capacity and the drive to change and to become fitter, stronger, leaner, and higher educated, with higher-value skill sets.

And what about the consumer versus the worker debate? As consumers, we love Wal-Mart's lower prices, giving us access to a wider range of products that we couldn't previously afford. As a worker, these lower prices are being delivered by the same outsourcing and offshoring that are causing us to lose our jobs.

China and India are not the problem. *We* are the problem. Our inability to construct a basic values system where we understand the importance of retraining, reskilling, and re-equipping people for the challenges that lie ahead is our failing. In my 2008 Philanthropy and Development class at St. Mary's University, in Minnesota, one of my students hailed from Flint, Michigan. Steve was the development director in a Flint elementary school. During the class he shared some horrific realities about one of the United States' most depressed and abandoned cities, which has been out on a limb since the decline of the traditional American automotive industry began a decade or so ago. High school students had a 25 percent graduation rate. The crime rate was into the stratosphere. Prospects had hit rock bottom, as had the population, which had been leaving in droves. Steve was convinced that education was the key. But it was criminally underfunded. So, yet again, the third sector was filling the gap. Steve decided that his elementary school would spearhead a campaign to "Save Flint." At the time of writing, documentary filmmaker Michael Moore had expressed a firm interest and Steve was working closely with his classmates from St. Mary's to look at how to develop and implement the campaign.

The Flat World

This chronic failing of Western economies to prioritize education and reskilling has left cities like Flint, or Sheffield in the UK, or Tourcoing in France at the mercy of the outsourcing economic reality. No wonder people in such places are scared of globalization—we have failed to give them the tools to see it otherwise.

To return to the economic reasons behind globalization, there is another that merits some serious thought from our sector.

Supply chaining is the art, as much as the science, of coordinating a number of different suppliers to ensure that a product arrives in front of the customer at the right time, in the right place, and in the right condition. I argue that it is as much an art as a science because a well-constructed and well-executed supply chain has a sense of the art that you find in a good soccer game, when all the players seem to move independently, but as one, in order to achieve one goal. Commercial organizations such as Dell, Wal-Mart, and Amazon owe their success less to their marketing or branding than to their ability to optimize and maximize their supply chains to gain valuable percentage points in efficiency, which they then pass on to their clients.

Supply chains are absolutely, totally global. When you order a computer online from Dell, the different components that will end up in your PC box will be sourced from as many as 50 different suppliers in over 10 different countries—from Europe to China, via Taiwan, India, and many, many others. Their success depends on total stability throughout the supply chain—both political and economic stability. And as we shall see later in this book, this desire for stability could well be one of the influencing factors in balancing out the flat philanthropic world in the years to come.

But the nonprofit world has not been left behind. Emergency relief organizations have upscaled their supply chains in order to be able to react in record time to crises, wherever they happen to be.

The Three Tippers

The human, technological, political, and economic factors help to explain some of the big globalization trends, but in themselves they are not enough to have caused the huge changes we have been experiencing over the past 5 to 10 years. They needed to come together at some point and reach a moment of confluence, or a "tipping point," as Malcolm Gladwell puts it in his seminal book. So what was the tipping point that brought these together to unleash such overwhelming change on the world?

Thomas Friedman argues that there are three factors that have contributed and come together at a certain time to tip the scales. I agree with the fact that there are three, but believe very strongly that one of these is far and away the most prominent and most important.

First is broadband. Globalization relies on technology to support its interactions. And technology relies on wires in the ground to support its interactions. The Internet is sterile if no one can access it, and it will have no information on it (and therefore no value) if people do not have the bandwidth to be able to share their digitized content. Just look at the correlation between growth of online purchasing (and giving) and broadband connectivity.

Second is inertia. More than 40 years elapsed between the invention of the lightbulb and the widespread availability of electric lights in Western houses. There is always a time lag in technology, produced both by a lack of infrastructure and by the fact that people need time to adjust and integrate technology. Think how long it took some people to work out how to set a VCR player. Think about the fact that the tin can was invented five years before the tin can opener!

But the third and most important factor is that we suddenly unleashed the talent, the determination, and the energy of three billion people!

In 1985, the global economic world (North America, Western Europe, Japan, parts of Asia and Latin America) comprised 2.5 billion people. During the 1990s, the economies of China, Russia, India, Eastern Europe, and Central Asia all opened up—a new market of 3 billion potential consumers, hungry consumers. And even if only 150 million have current access to the market and can be considered to be on the same wealth level as the Western economic world, that is still more than half of the U.S. market in terms of numbers of consumers.

These three billion are hungry people. They are hungry to take our place—not to be us, but to be better than us! And these new economies have understood something that we have underestimated for a long time—and I lamented earlier in this chapter: they have understood the importance of education.

India sent more university students to the United States in 2004 and 2005 than any other country (over 80,000, with 62,000 from China). Previously these students were graduating and then staying in the United States and going to work for companies like Goldman Sachs. Now they are going back to India and working for companies like Goldman Sachs! Each year the United States trains some 150,000 Indians and Chinese to lead the companies that will be at the forefront of the next stage of this globalized revolution.

The Exponential World

The speed with which this is happening is overwhelming. The first commercial use of text messaging took place in December 1992. Today, whatever day it is that you are reading this, the number of text messages sent will exceed the number of human beings on the planet. This month, Google will receive nearly three billion searches and MySpace will have another 230,000 members.

This is change—big time. And it is not slowing down. Quite the opposite. We have entered the exponential world. In the exponential world, change does not just have a percentage-point, incremental increase. It has a doubling, tripling increase. EBay was created in 1996. The exponential world has allowed its revenue to grow to $6 billion in just a dozen years.

The world is flat and exponential, and as fundraisers we have to first understand this concept and then apply it to our work. It is no longer good enough to achieve four- to five-point increases in direct marketing revenue year to year. Our mission requires more. Our beneficiaries deserve more. We are being demanded to do more. But just maybe, for the first time ever, we now have the tools to do more. The gauntlet is down and the choice is ours: do we pick it up and make the most of this incredible opportunity, or do we allow it to pass us by?

The Flat World

Exponential growth also brings with it some intriguing questions, like where did we obtain those billions of bits of information each month before Google? And, in the words of Clinton advisor David Rothkopf, "What happens if the political entity in which you are located no longer corresponds to a job that takes place in cyberspace, or no longer really encompasses workers collaborating with other workers in different corners of the globe, or no longer really captures products produced in multiple places simultaneously? Who regulates the work? Who taxes it? Who should benefit from those taxes?"

Increasingly, we are going to have to face up to the fact that we don't have the answers. We may only have the questions. And this is a fundamental change to the way we think and work as organizations. Nonprofits are risk-averse by nature. But we are going to have to turn that around and realize that if we only act according to a set of rules that are tried and proven, we are robbing ourselves and our beneficiaries of a real chance. In a sense, we are preventing ourselves from being the organizations we could be, preventing our beneficiaries from receiving the help and support they need, and preventing our missions from being fulfilled.

Quantum physics is all about taking giant leaps into the unknown, testing and proving. Today we need quantum fundraising—where we throw out the rule book, encourage failure, test new things, promote research and development, and do this in absolute transparency with our donors with the aim of sharing an ambitious vision to do ourselves out of a job. If you are a fundraiser, your job just changed. You are no longer a philanthropy developer; you are a philanthropy revolutionary. Your aim is exponential fundraising, where growth and mission accomplishment are driven by innovation and change. Henry Ford said, "Whether you think that you can, or that you think you can't, you are usually right." Your aim is quantum fundraising, where you throw the rule book away and put absolute faith in your vision for change. Lack of self-confidence has no place in the fundraising world of tomorrow. The stakes are too high. Too many people are depending on us. If you don't believe you can change the world, get out of the game. If you do believe you can change the world, make it happen; then tell us about it.

The Flat World

Quantum fundraising is going to be our Red Bull for the flat philanthropic world. It is going to pump us full of energy and send us off in the right direction. It is going to help us deal with the three big challenges that are coming right at us like a speeding truck: choice, individualism, and disappearing boundaries—the realities of the flat world.

Chapter Two

The Realities of the Flat World

Young Chinese, Indians, and Poles are not racing us to the bottom. They are racing us to the top. They do not want to work for us. They do not even want to be us. They want to dominate us—in the sense that they want to be creating the companies of the future, ones that people all over the world will admire and clamor to work for. They are in no way content with where they have come so far. . . . [Bill] Gates is recognized everywhere he goes in China.

Young people there hang from the rafters and scalp tickets just to hear him speak. Same with Jerry Yang, the co-founder of Yahoo!

In China today, Bill Gates is Britney Spears. In America today, Britney Spears is Britney Spears—and that is our problem.

—Thomas Friedman, *The World Is Flat*

As we have already seen, globalization, exponential change, and the big, wild, wacky flat world are having huge effects on us all. They are affecting every part of our lives, every day of the week. And their impact is being felt globally, from the richest to the poorest countries. Very few countries, communities, or individuals have not felt a direct or indirect, positive or negative impact of the flat world. But what are these different impacts? How can we try to sort some sense into this, to understand it better in order to know how to deal with it more effectively? We cannot, after all, pick up the gauntlet if we don't know what it looks like and how much it weighs.

There are no doubt hundreds, maybe even thousands, of micro and macro impacts of globalization, which vary according to culture, community, and level of development. However, for this book I have done some serious culling and bunching to try to bring them down to a manageable number that we can deal with and integrate quickly and effectively into our fundraising strategy and thinking. As the U.S. soul group DelaSoul put it back in the late 1980s, "Three is the magic number." So that shall be our guide.

Choice

We talked in the previous chapter about how anyone, given access to a camera phone with a recording device and the Web, can now be a journalist. This democratization is not limited to news and media. On the contrary, everything we do in the flat world is characterized by immense choice. "Whether we like it or not, we are all citizens of a world dominated by markets. We are surrounded by the mania of markets and live in a society where money is meaning, where freedom does not always equal happiness and where technological opportunity does not always lead to profits."—Jonas Ridderstrale and Kjell Nordstrom, Karaoke Capitalism.

Markets now control everything we do, everything in our lives. As Thomas Friedman puts it, "Independent journalism and its relative, blogging, are expressions of market forces—a need not being met by current information sources."

What about fundraising? Are we choice-driven? Of course we are! Or at least our donors are. In the United States today there are more than 900,000 nonprofits, all out for the same donor dollars. In France the number of registered charities is even higher, somewhere around the million mark, and although few are currently actively fundraising, they all have the legal capacity to do so.

A few years ago, we would give our money to people who asked for it. We would have our community charities, or our development nonprofits that we would support regularly with either a monthly gift or a regular donation at the end of the year. But then the world flattened, and suddenly we realized how many organizations there were, how much choice we had.

Organizations started vying for our attention, with sexier, more interesting campaigns. Some even started showing how our donor dollars could make a real difference. Some told more stories. Others communicated with us in the way that we wanted them to, for the first time, allowing us to receive e-mails rather than phone calls, and to choose when we received them.

As in every other market, the flattening of the world has increased competition and turned the customer into what Jonas Ridderstrale and Kjell Nordstrom call in their book *Karaoke Capitalism,* a "demanding dictator."

And what happened? Donors started to want to choose who they gave their money to on the basis of criteria that they were deciding on instead of us deciding for them.

Enter Guidestar, Charity Navigator, and the start of what is becoming a nonprofit transparency revolution. Charity rating web sites are much maligned, both in the United States and in Europe where various projects are currently being developed, but without doubt they are a very powerful tool for both donors and nonprofits (if we used it more!). In the United States, Guidestar, Charity Navigator, and others are simply a system that builds on the American tax office's annual required information submissions by nonprofits in order to make them available to the public through the Web. Financial information is available for all to see, and a search and rating system has been developed to allow the potential donor in the blink of an eye and a couple of clicks to identify charities in his or her chosen field (children, local community, education . . .) and then see which are the best performers.

Whether the criteria for performance are judged to be credible is a debate that merits more space than this book can give, but the real innovation is the ability of each nonprofit to comment, explain, and provide further information on itself. This is truly revolutionary, and totally empowering for both the donor and the charity. If you are going through a period of intense development and investment to grow your organization to a stage where it will be able to take on a bigger mission tomorrow, you can explain this to donors. You can share your strategic plan and explain how funds are being reinvested—educate through the ratios. And donors can access this information and decide for themselves whether you are worthy of support.

The Realities of the Flat World

In the United States, increasing numbers of giving decisions are now being made after having consulted a charity rating web site. And we can transform Thomas Friedman's quote on independent journalism to refer to this phenomenon without too much trouble: "*Independent donor decision making and its relative, Guidestar et al.,* are expressions of market forces—a need not being met by current information sources."

These web sites and their empowering nature have themselves fueled the exponential circle. Because more people use Guidestar, because more nonprofits post information on it, its value and its reach grow exponentially. This creates more need, and in turn attracts more donors and nonprofits. It is a transparency circle—a circle of more transparency, leading to more need, leading to more supply of information, leading to more value, leading to more transparency.

If the three stages of globalization are characterized respectively by the questions "How can my country, my company, and myself go global?" maybe fundraising is now being characterized by the move from "How can I help my charity?" to "How can I help with charity?" And nowhere is this being seen more clearly than in the growth of community, family, and new individual foundations across the world.

Without going into the whole history of community and individual foundations, a few years ago we started seeing a serious trend of rich individuals deciding to take philanthropy into their own hands. Increasingly unhappy about the growing number of solicitations from an ever-larger number of needy causes, these individuals began to take the initiative, often grouping together to decide where their money should go in order to increase the real impact.

However, reading between the lines, their real message to fundraisers and nonprofits was "We've had enough of getting hassled by an ever-growing number of you guys, giving to you, and then never really finding out what the money is being used for and how well it's being used. So we're going to get together and create our own foundations. We are going to choose which organizations we give our money to. And we're going to do it in a much more professional and business-minded way than you are." A study in the United Kingdom recently noted that fundraisers were less trusted than realtors. This is *not* good news!

The Realities of the Flat World

I don't think we fundraisers and nonprofits have taken this message seriously enough. In fact, I think that a great number of us really don't want to hear it. Sure, we have improved our professionalism as a sector on a global level in the past few years—we are more transparent and effective—but we are often still pretty amateurish. If a major company had half of its new customers leave within 12 months, they'd be going out of business pretty quickly, but that is the reality for a great many nonprofits around the world.

So rich people started taking things into their own hands, and we increasingly had to apply to their foundations for funding, rather than just nurturing and stewarding individual relationships. Think Bill and Melinda Gates. Even more so, think Warren Buffett. And it was the flat world that provided the tools and the availability of information necessary to do all this.

But then this trend of total choice and empowerment through the flat world soon spread out of the domain of the mega-rich and started hitting the ordinary joes of this world—the people who give for a variety of different reasons, and who probably nowadays increasingly go from one organization to another.

And, again, the flat world provided the tools to allow this need—the need for everyday donors to have more choice in their philanthropy—to be met. Firstgiving. com was created in 2003 (see Exhibit 2.1). A total revolution in giving, it simply allows any individual to go online and within a matter of minutes create a personalized home page with a built-in online giving module and then send out a link to an e-mail address book. As of late 2008, more than 1.3 million people have used it to raise over $74 million for more than 15,000 different nonprofits.

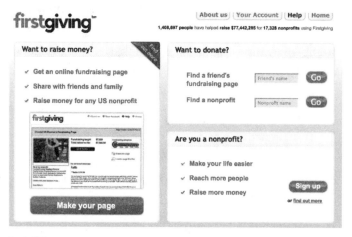

Exhibit 2.1   Firstgiving.com Web Site

The Realities of the Flat World

Let's just stop for a moment and think about this. A web site has suddenly given every individual the opportunity to not only choose the charity that they want to support, but also the technology to be able to invite all their friends to support it, too—and from the comfort of their desktop PC. Who needs direct mail in a world like this?

After all, as an individual who believes in philanthropy, how does one choose causes to give to? Probably Mr. and Ms. Individual will have a couple of favorite charities that they give to pretty regularly. And then the rest are just on an "as and when" basis, either when they see a campaign or when they hear about something in the news . . . or when one of their friends tells them about a favorite charity.

Because what is more powerful than a recommendation from a friend? Arguably, nothing. Indeed, many corporations with advertising budgets that would make most fundraisers weep are now spending more and more time and effort trying to get peers to recommend their products (hence the interest in bloggers). I first discovered Justgiving.org when I received an e-mail from my friend Sarah. The e-mail went something like this:

"Dear Jon [*nice personalized entry point!*],

"I hope you are well, and thanks for taking the time to read this e-mail. You know that for a long time I have been a supporter of X charity and the work they do across the country. This is why I have decided to participate in their annual sponsored Triathlon next month. I am training really hard to be able to get fit enough in time. Please click here to visit my Triathlon home page, and please do take a minute to sponsor me online. Thanks so much, and I look forward to seeing you soon.

"Love, Sarah"

This was a personalized e-mail. A friendly e-mail. So I clicked. Two minutes later I was back on my spreadsheet having sponsored Sarah and made an online donation. Would I have made a donation to this charity if Sarah had not asked me? No. Would I have reacted to a mailpack or a campaign by the charity? Well, they'd sent me a few in the previous months and I hadn't replied to any, so the answer has to again be no. This is the power of the individual and of social networking. And it has been made possible by the flat world platform.

The Realities of the Flat World

Individuals are empowering themselves, or are being empowered by flat world tools, to take fundraising into their own hands. Social networking tools are perhaps the newest and sexiest to arrive, and as technology develops they will certainly become more subtle, more integrated, and more effective—allowing the donor to have almost unlimited choice over his or her fundraising activities. It is no longer a question of simply asking donors for money. We now have to entice them to our cause and empower them with the tools to make a difference— their way. In the same way as Burger King promises to make your Whopper "your way" (i.e., without those horrible gherkins), we now have to work out what it is to make a donation "your way." Each organization is going to have a different entry point, but one thing is for sure: If we try to force fundraising gherkins on our donors, they are going to go somewhere else. The gauntlet is down, and the choice is theirs.

This is just one more example of how biography is the new geography. Ignore it at your peril.

And then, just when we thought that democracy and choice in fundraising couldn't get any worse, along came

Hurricane Katrina. I will spend some more time on the impact of this catastrophe on fundraising in a later chapter, but for now let's look at what happened on a purely pragmatic level. Katrina was the biggest peer-to-peer catastrophe to hit a Western country for a good decade. What do we mean by peer-to-peer? Well, in the same way as you might share your music files (illegally, for the moment, of course) with other individuals over the flat world platform that is the Internet, individuals after Katrina started to share their possessions and their giving with others. Once the initial period of shock and lawlessness abated and some semblance of order was restored, we saw an incredible amount of person-to-person solidarity: friends helping friends. Communities helping each other. Neighbors helping other neighbors. Relatives taking care of relatives.

This peer-to-peer solidarity was more often than not completely unorchestrated and untouched by organized philanthropy. It was just people helping people.

But in the flat world, anything that can be done offline can be done online (well, almost . . .). And so it was that web sites like Modestneeds.org started to flourish. Modestneeds.org allows individuals in the United States who are going through hard times to call upon the financial support of total strangers to help them get back on their feet. It is pure donor-to-beneficiary philanthropy—the online equivalent of putting a big packet of dollars directly into someone's hand.

Since it began, Modestneeds claims to have facilitated changes in the lives of more than 3,500 people. Actually, Modestneeds doesn't claim that *it* has changed anything. It claims simply that 3,500 individuals have changed the lives of 3,500 other individuals by giving them money. In 2006, more than $500,000 transited through the web site.

Again, let's take a moment to reflect on this. Modestneeds flies absolutely and totally in the face of all established fundraising theory. "What about the controls on use of funds?" we ask. "What about transparency and giving according to real needs?" we protest. "What about trust and confidence, the vital statistics of fundraising success?" we cry! This goes against all thinking on trust and confidence. How can you possibly trust or have confidence in an individual whom you have never met? How can you be confident when there is no track record? When there is no way of telling if the funds have been used appropriately?

However, thousands of people are using this service. They are logging on and transferring funds to other people who appear to have a need. They are peer-to-peer fundraising. There is no middleman. No third party. No nonprofit. Why they are doing this is a good question, and one that would merit an in-depth study of Modestneeds' donor motivations. However, I would hazard a guess that actually most individuals have a good soul, and want to make the world a better place. And that, despite what the media and certain politicians would like us to believe, asking for someone's charity is something that the vast majority of human beings do only when they really have no other choice. It is not something most of us do easily, and as a result, there is a fundamental filtering process happening. The donors want to do good, and increasingly want to see the tangible results of their gifts. They may even want to create links with the beneficiaries in a similar way to being a child sponsor. And the beneficiaries really need the support and appreciate it.

Let's be clear here; this is still a very minority activity . . . for the moment. At the time of writing, only 3,500 people have been helped by Modestneeds. But it is not the only web site providing such peer-to-peer fundraising opportunities. I believe the flat world is going to be increasingly powerful in bringing together individuals with needs and individuals with the capacity to give—in other words, in bringing together the two markets of nonprofits without the nonprofit in the middle. By cutting us out, the donor wins by ensuring that all of his or her money goes to the beneficiary. And the beneficiary wins by having the opportunity to create a relationship with the donor.

It is safe to say we have not seen the end of this trend.

Individualism

The world is a weird place, never quite easy to understand and always full of surprises. Who would have thought, for example, that in a world where we have almost limitless choice, people would start to become more individualistic?

But irony aside, huge choice is producing huge individualism. *Me* has replaced any semblance of *us* in many Western societies. Children spend more and more hours in front of video games and on the Internet, fulfilling *me* needs rather than interacting with other kids and building social and supportive communities. Adults have taken things even further. Think of our difficulties in abandoning private cars in favor of public transport, despite the fact that the average speed in many cities these days is lower than it was when we used horses and carts. Think of our desire to be considered by business and customer service centers as individuals. We have entered a world where we all want to be considered in a segment of one: me!

The baby boom generation, which is moving massively toward retirement like an out-of-control ship toward an iceberg, is the epitome of this incredible hedonism. Travel companies in the United States specializing in the over-50 markets now talk about proposing SKI-ing holidays to their customers. Not such a surprise, you may say. Over-50s are now fitter than ever; why shouldn't they enjoy heading down a mountain every so often? Except the SKI-ing holidays that these companies are referring to are Spending the Kids' Inheritance holidays. Welcome to the "I've earned it, I'm spending it" generation.

The Realities of the Flat World

The chance to tap into this generational spending spree does, of course, represent an incredible opportunity for nonprofits. But we need to be smarter, sharper, and more donor-centered to make this happen. Today, how many nonprofits can realistically say that they treat their supporters in segments of one? But tomorrow, if we want a slice of this huge baby boomer chocolate and cream cake with cherries on top, we are going to have to fundamentally change our thinking and our practices.

Both Simone Joyaux (*Beyond Fundraising*, Wiley, 2005) and Kay Sprinkel Grace (*Keep Your Donors*, Wiley, 2007) two of the most visionary leaders in nonprofit thinking, have spoken and written at length on how to develop donor-centered fundraising. This author will not attempt to do even the palest imitation of their work, but feels strongly that the huge value that can be gained from putting the donor and supporter at the heart of the organization—both figuratively and in reality—makes it worthwhile to read their books soon.

Tomorrow (and this should come as good news for anti-globalizationers everywhere), global trade and economics and development are going to be less and less in the hands of the World Trade Organization, the World

Bank, and the G-8. Individuals who have understood the flat world, who are adapting quickly to its processes and technologies, and who are starting to innovate and create value horizontally rather than through the traditional vertical organizations are going to be the ones with the power. I'm afraid it's true—the geeks really are going to inherit the earth.

Back in the 1980s we had the yuppies, then the NIMBYs (not in my backyard), and ever since a plethora of abbreviations to try to systematize cultural trends. However, the cultural trends of tomorrow are all pointing toward a new group, a segment not of one but of millions, who are positioning themselves today to occupy some of the world's most powerful positions tomorrow. They are called the zippies, or as the Indian weekly magazine *Outlook* calls them, "Liberalization's Children." Thomas Friedman quotes the magazine's definition of a zippie as a "young city or suburban resident, between 15 and 25, with a zip in the stride. Belongs to generation Z. . . . Cool, confident and creative. Seeks challenges, loves risks and shuns fear."

As cute as this may sound, it takes on a whole other meaning when you consider that more than half of the Indian population is under 25.

The Realities of the Flat World

The zippies, not just from India, but also from China, from Eastern and Central Europe, even from Western Europe and North America, will tomorrow not just be running business and nonprofit empires with new, totally global models; it is entirely possible that they will be directly influencing most of the vital elements of the planet's economic and social makeup in ways that tomorrow's national leaders will only be able to dream of. Through supply chaining, horizontal collaboration, virtual networks, and the flat world Web platform, and by breaking down boundaries between cultures and nations, these global village children are going to be changing our perspectives on our planet. Please fasten your seatbelt. We are cleared for takeoff.

One of the trends underpinning the thinking behind this book, as you will have already understood, is the huge importance of the individual in the flat world. The responsibility is in our hands—not those of our governments, of our society leaders, or of intellectuals. When I was at school, we used to sing a hymn that began "He has the whole world in his hands," referring to the power of the Almighty. Without wishing to offend any religious sensibilities, there is a distinct possibility

81

that the children of tomorrow could be singing the same song, but replacing *He has* by *You have.*

Alexander Bard and Jan Söderqvist, authors of *The Global Empire,* make some very interesting challenges to the concept of the individual. According to their book, as we become increasingly individualistic and concentrate more on our own personal satisfaction through our choices, the traditional *individual* will eventually be replaced by the slightly schizophrenic *dividual.* This is someone who harbors a number of different personalities and who functions in various tribal networks, according to biography rather than geography, and defines traits of personality differently in each network.

I would like to argue that this change is already happening, and in a big way. We already compartmentalize our physical lives into a number of different boxes. We have work, with relationships with colleagues; family, with relationships with our wives, husbands, partners, and kids; sport, with relationships with golfing or gym friends; volunteering, with relationships with other volunteers or board members. . . .

Many of us take pleasure in segmenting our lives in such a way. We want our family time away from our colleagues, and often have behavior and personality traits that are differentiated according to the various networks we are in. The virtual world just allows us to take this one stage further. As an interesting illustration of this, let's look at gender. Few of us change gender, or give the impression of changing gender through physical presentation, according to our networks. It is pretty unlikely that you will pretend to be a man at work, but play golf as a woman. However, the Web and the flat world networks allow us to do this. We can be whoever we want to be behind the avatars of our Web personalities. We can be women or men, black or white, big or small. Just look at Second Life (it is claimed that a surprisingly large number of men use female avatars, and vice versa, in online gaming and in Second Life for example). Ultimately, the authors of *The Global Empire* claim, we could move from wanting therapy because we have multiple personalities to having therapy because we don't have enough!

Again, this is something that, as nonprofits, we need to be aware of. It will not revolutionize the way we work tomorrow, but it is one further factor that we need to have integrated into our fundraising. Not only will we have to consider donors as segments of one, but we will increasingly have to diversify the number of segments to deal with the different personality traits that an individual wants to share with us. No longer can we consider that Dorothy Donors all look alike. Dorothy may be at the gym, with her family, in a chat room, at work, or anywhere else. And she will want different things from us according to where she is. Fundraising just got a bit more complicated!

Disappearing Boundaries

We have seen in the past few chapters a number of references to horizontal collaboration as a way of adding value to our organizations. This new way of thinking and working is possible only because the flat world is constantly pushing back boundaries and allowing people to interact and collaborate in ways never before available. Corporations are becoming foundations, foundations are becoming multinationals, donors are becoming nonprofits, and nonprofits are becoming donors. Whatever was impossible yesterday is possible today and is downright likely tomorrow.

The Realities of the Flat World

Tom Friedman tells the story of Rajesh Rao, founder of Dhruva Interactive, a small game company based in Bangalore. Having started the company in 1995 with a bank loan for a computer and a modem, he set out to become a supplier of quality outsourcing to the U.S. and European markets.

Ten years later, this start-up Indian company bought the rights to use Charlie Chaplin's image for computer games. An Indian company now owns one of Western cinema's greatest icons.

But Rajesh Rao (another example of an Indian zippie) is not alone in breaking down boundaries. Médecins sans Frontières (MSF) has been doing it for nearly two decades. Founded by a team of doctors that included Bernard Kouchner, now the French foreign affairs minister, the international nonprofit has always been associated with unorthodox, boundary-free activity, living and thriving according to its very strong and militant values. These doctors produced a huge outcry back in 2005 when they publicly asked donors to stop giving after the Asian tsunami, an issue that we address in later chapters. But MSF has also been blurring a very interesting boundary between charity and media for a number of years. When you receive an MSF recruitment mailing in France, the United Kingdom, the United States, or any of the other countries they are present in, you could be forgiven for thinking that you've been sent a news magazine. They recruit on content, on the in-your-face, "direct from our own correspondents," tell-it-like-it-is image. They communicate on the reality of the world today, and give information on places and events that rarely make CNN.

Donors give to MSF because they want to know what is happening in the world. They don't trust Rupert Murdoch and cable TV to give it to them. They trust MSF.

MSF is a part of today's media. And more than that, it is a trusted source within the media (almost an oxymoron in our flat world days).

But is it just charities that are blurring boundaries? Unfortunately for us, no.

The corporate world has latched onto the fact that nonprofit values sell. Businesses have understood this and are throwing resources at it in a huge way.

Aspirations are the future, and corporations have seen the value in nonprofit. Think of Dove, a soap brand from one of the largest industrial multinationals in the world, Unilever. In 2005, the Dove brand launched the "Campaign for Real Beauty," a militant-style advertising brand concept that was designed to encourage women to express their beauty without having to conform to society's stereotypes. It was a stunning piece of communication, which very cleverly used the flat world tools and aspirations with huge success. The campaign created a virtual worldwide community of women, brought the issue of catwalk-style waiflike beauty to the fore of public debate, and of course, increased the sales of Dove soap.

But such a move into the world of nonprofit values marketing would not have been complete without the creation of some kind of fund to *walk the talk*. And so was created the Dove Self-Esteem fund to provide resources for projects that would work with girls and young women suffering from eating disorders as a result of society's waiflike projection of idealized beauty.

When this campaign came out, I was worried. Very worried. Here was one of the largest multinationals taking over nonprofit values, launching a campaign, of all things. Amnesty and Greenpeace launch campaigns, not Procter & Gamble with Unilever! This truly was a company being a charity in a way we had never seen before. Suddenly charities had moved from being an indispensable part of society to being an expendable middleman. Business could do it without us.

But then I started to research the campaign and see its impact, and my anxiety turned to respect. They were really good. Yes, Unilever hijacked nonprofit communication territory, and to a certain extent showed the nonprofit world that business didn't really need us; but, boy, were they doing it well! They had done their research and discovered that there were no global brands in the eating disorder territory. They had managed to build a huge social network community of hundreds of thousands of women around the globe. They had even managed to include an online donations page on their web site. Yes, to be fair, they were doing it with global advertising budgets that would feed a large part of Africa, but even so. Awareness of the issue they were out to promote was rising, brand loyalty was rising, women were having positive images sent through the media rather than the self-esteem-destroying images that adorn fashion magazines—and Dove's sales were rising. My instant reaction of outrage at a multinational trampling all over our values to increase sales and profits to its shareholders began to turn to a big question: what if the flat world started to really blur the line between corporate and nonprofit and bring with it huge opportunity for the good guys (us!)?

The flat world *is* bringing opportunity, in new and exciting ways. One of those opportunities will be for corporations to develop socially responsible and non-profit activities that deliver services to the community and may even raise funds while at the same time selling more products and making more money. Capital for good, in a word.

But another of these opportunities will allow charities to develop for-profit activities and income-generation streams that allow us to compete with corporations by using their values branding and their status as a sales argument. If I had a choice of airlines between a traditional, for-profit corporation and a nonprofit organization that plowed its profits back into the environment, I know which one I'd choose. It's just that I don't have the choice—yet.

And this really is the fundamental message here. The world has changed and the playing field has been shaken up. Eventually, if it is not already happening, your organization is going to be competing with others who are out to make a buck. They will often be more aggressive, have larger budgets, and be capital-driven. They are going to try to take your market share, because market share = profit. So we need to fight back. And we need to use what has always distinguished the nonprofit from the for-profit sector—our creativity. Fundraisers are seemingly born with the natural capacity to do less with more in a way that corporations, when they examine the way we work, find difficult to believe. Because we have no money, we need to rely on our creativity. We need to be guerrillas, challenging and fresh.

And we need to identify niche markets where we can offer products and services that people will buy because they are good things. Then we need to develop business models to make it happen. And a recent study in France showed that 82 percent of customers would rather buy a product, given equal price and quality, from a responsible supplier. People will prefer your product. Think fair trade coffee.

The boundaries are disappearing, and again we are faced with a choice. Either we stick our heads in the sand and pretend that it is not happening, or we wait to see what it will mean for us, or we anticipate and develop. If your organization chooses one of the first two, it might be time to start looking for a new job.

One other result of the erosion of boundaries in the flat philanthropic world is the increasing amount of information that we have. Instead of trusting traditional media, we now have the choice to check out blogs written by individuals or web sites created by charities like MSF. Instead of giving money to the charities that write to us, we can give to the charities that our friends recommend, or even give directly to those in need. But increasingly, the fact that the information exists doesn't necessarily mean that we know what to do with it when we receive it. An emerging problem in health care in the United States is people self-diagnosing themselves using Google. We have information, but we don't necessarily have knowledge.

This brings us back to the idea of moving from the "information age" to the "talent age." What talent does is turn information into knowledge. If you want to know how to identify and penetrate niche markets for new products that you can deliver to potential consumers, you need to know how to make sense of the vast quantities of information out there to guide your choices and strategy. And for that you need talent.

Data can become information without talent. But information cannot become knowledge and be applied to create additional value without talent. And in order to thrive and survive in the flat philanthropic world, we need to better understand this. And more importantly, we actually need to apply it.

And we should take heed of this story from Tom Friedman in *The World Is Flat* when thinking about whether we are really equipped to deal with the information we are confronted with:

> *Mark Steyn, writing in the* National Review *(October 25, 2004), related a story from the London Arabic newspaper* Al-Quds al-Arabi *about a panic that broke out in Khartoum, Sudan, after a crazy rumor swept the city, claiming that if an infidel shook a man's hand, that man could lose his manhood. "What struck me about the story,"*

wrote Steyn, "was a detail: *The hysteria was spread by cell phones and text messaging. Think about that: You can own a cell phone yet still believe a foreigner's handshake can melt away your penis. What happens when that kind of technologically advanced primitivism advances beyond text messaging?"*

Chapter Three

The Global Philanthropy Crisis

Middle-Class Heroes

In [a] state of natural liberty, society will be their first thought. A thousand motives will excite them thereto, the strength of one man is so unequal to his wants, and his mind so unfitted for perpetual solitude, that he is soon obliged to seek assistance and relief of another, who in his turn requires the same. Four or five united would be able to raise a tolerable dwelling in the midst of a wilderness, but one man might labour out the common period of life without accomplishing any thing.

—Thomas Paine

Philanthropy has always been with us. People's capacity to act as societal beings and to share, philanthropically, their energies, talents, and capacities for the greater good is one of the underlying factors of humanity. And Thomas Paine, the English-born American political pamphleteer, expresses it very clearly in the preceding quote from his 1776 "Common Sense" essay.

Jerry Yang, the co-founder of Yahoo!, once quoted a Chinese senior government official saying, "Where you have hope, you have a middle class." This is a fantastic quote, one that sums up perfectly the situation today in China and in many fast-developing economies populated by zippies. In fact, I like this quote so much I have amended it to "Where you have hope, you have a middle class. *Where you have a middle class, you have philanthropy.*"

As we look around the flat philanthropic world, from India and China to Australia, Japan, Eastern and Western Europe, and the Americas, what do we see?

The same trend. Entrepreneurism and economic openness lead to developing wealth, which in turn feeds political stability and allows people to advance socially. This is the capitalist model. And it allows individuals and communities to progress through up Abraham Maslow's Needs Pyramid, accumulating wealth and stability as they go. As Maslow tells us, philanthropy can only really come once we have enough to provide for ourselves. This, as with every rule, goes only as far as its exceptions, but serves for most organizations involved in fundraising around the world. For most of our money does not come from the very rich or the very poor; it comes from the middle class. Philanthropy grows in direct correlation to the growth and the stability of the middle class.

The opening of economies from Russia to India and China in the past 15 years, has, as we have seen, brought billions more people into the global economy. True, only a very small percentage of them currently are able to purchase, consume, and give at the levels of a typical Westerner, but the scales are such that even a small percentage represents a huge bound for the world philanthropic economy.

Today, the ranks of the Indian middle class, the Chinese middle class, and the Eastern European middle class are experiencing solid, vibrant growth. And for the first time ever we are witnessing the flattening of the philanthropic world. In the flat philanthropic world, money is everywhere and nowhere at the same time. It is no longer true to say that there are rich countries and poor countries. There are richer and poorer countries, but there are increasingly sufficient financial philanthropic resources available in the poorer countries to fund projects and initiatives. We can no longer consider the fundraising world in terms of haves and have-nots. We can no longer satisfy ourselves with the idea that we raise money from the rich and give it to the poor. When the infant mortality rate in Washington, D.C., is 16.2 children out of every 1,000, a figure that equals that of Sri Lanka, or when the number of babies born underweight in the U.S. capital is higher than in Zambia, we have a global philanthropy crisis.

Where is the need? Where is the money? The need used to be social in the global North and developmental in the global South. The money used to be in the global North. Now both the money and the development needs are increasingly to be found everywhere.

The international fundraiser, Ken Burnett tells the story of a session that Bernard Ross, (founder of the Management Centre, a non-profit consultancy based in the UK) once ran, where a woman from a charity in Ethiopia first encountered direct marketing. She returned to Addis Ababa, the country's capital, to try it out, and received a nearly 40 percent response rate.

What is this telling us? It is first telling us that people in countries that have been traditionally nonfundraising countries are starting to move into fundraising. The Ukraine has just organized its seventh fundraising congress. Poland has just created a national fundraising association. Georgia just ran its first-ever fundraising conference. Hungary is creating a fundraising training certificate so that the profession can be recognized! Training and development in fundraising are happening across the globe, as the flat world increases the need and the opportunity to do incredible work funded locally. I have been lucky enough to be involved in some of these programs over the past few years, and have been blown away by the creativity and the drive of our new fundraising colleagues, many of whom had never heard of fundraising until very recently. These *new kids on the block* are the ones who are redefining our profession. They don't know the rules of fundraising, and there is nothing more powerful than someone who is determined and passionate, and doesn't know the rules.

The rules are there as a normative device for us, because most nonprofit organizations are naturally conservative, with boards who don't like taking risks. We know that if we follow X or Y fundraising technique, with a certain type of message addressed in a certain way to a certain type of audience, we will get Z result. QED.

The problem is that new and excited fundraisers don't know these norms, and they follow the best norm of all—passionate common sense. This is, in my view, the most powerful skill that any fundraiser can have, the most powerful tool in any philanthropic box. We must learn from them. The flat philanthropic world requires it.

We cannot talk about global philanthropy without talking about diaspora fundraising. It is one of the largest sources of untapped revenue for many nonprofit organizations (NPOs) around the world. We only have to look at the billions that are transferred through Western Union each year from emigrants who are making money in more developed economies and who are sending back money to keep their families alive.

What is interesting about diaspora is that it is starting to go back the other way, with flows of funds from rich Indian families to depressed Indian communities in the United Kingdom as an example. It is the same for Mexican funds into the United States. Again, the concept of the need being in India and the funds being in the UK, or the need being in Mexico and the funds being in the United States, is increasingly outdated. The flat philanthropic world has put an end to this.

How can we react to, and grow with, the opportunities presented by the flat philanthropic world? Are there tools and keys that we need to master to be effective as fundraisers in the world of tomorrow? The answer to this question is a most resounding *yes*. There are things that we all need to integrate, concepts that we need to work with, and reflexes that we need to develop. We are going to explore these in the second part of this book, but before doing this there is one fundamental question that needs to be asked on the relationship between nonprofits and development.

The World Bank publishes figures on the estimated number of people in various countries and regions living on less than $1 per day. Let's compare these figures for China, South Asia (including India), and sub-Saharan Africa, three completely different regions being affected by globalization in very different ways.

China
1990: 375 million Chinese living on < $1 per day
2001: 212 million
2015: on the basis of current trends 16 million

South Asia: India, Pakistan, and Bangladesh
1990: 462 million
2001: 431 million
2015: on the basis of current trends 216 million

Sub-Saharan Africa
1990: 227 million
2001: 313 million
2015: on the basis of current trends 340 million

Why?

What explains this? Can we pin down a number of factors? Can we try to isolate what is keeping Africa from its potential? This book, or this author, does not have the pretension to believe that it can offer any solutions to global development issues that are being worked on and tested by hundreds of thousands of professionals around the world. However, I do believe that we can gain a deeper understanding of the African situation by learning from some of Thomas Friedman's work.

Development and Flatness

In *The World Is Flat,* Friedman argues that there are three keys to succeeding as a country in a flat world.

First, you need the infrastructure to connect people to the flat world: Internet, phones, roads, airports, and so on.

Second, you need education to get people innovating and collaborating.

Third, you need strong governance both on a local and on a national level to ensure that individuals have a stable playing field from which to innovate and develop.

This list may or may not be exhaustive, but it does have the advantage of giving us a guide to look at our activities as nonprofits. And when we do this, there are a couple of striking things. Let's start with infrastructure.

International development nongovernmental organizations (NGOs) do a huge amount of work in providing basic infrastructure, such as wells, access to drinking water, and in some cases telecommunications. But when I asked one of my students at St. Mary's University (Minnesota) Philanthropy and Development program—an incredible gentleman named Benyam Addis from Ethiopia, what his country most needed, his answer was unequivocal: roads. Are international nonprofits spending donor dollars building roads? I did some research on a dozen or so major international organizations and couldn't find much, if any information on the subject. Does that mean we are not building roads, when people clearly think it would be the best investment? And I imagine that not very many nonprofits are involved in creating airports. . . .

What about education? This is something that hundreds of development nonprofits are covering at a grassroots level, all across the world. But if we look at the countries that are pulling themselves out of poverty, such as India and China, where are they investing their education budgets? Not in grassroots schooling, but in universities. There is a key question here: is it in a population's best interests to have everybody educated to the age of 7, or to have a small number of people educated to MBA level? Should we be concentrating our work on making macro rather than micro educational decisions? Is it in the best interests of a society to abandon some children to illiteracy? And if so, who has the right to make such a decision? Is it our responsibility as citizens of the flat world? Is it the individual's responsibility? Is it the government's responsibility?

And what about governance? Most development nonprofits have some kind of Global South lobbying programs, but why are we not seeing more NGOs attacking the root causes of ineffective governance in places like Africa or South Asia? Why do we not hear more about this? Is it not sexy? Aside from a handful of organizations such as Amnesty International, Transparency, and Oxfam, which lobby hard and push governance as a key mission issue, as donors, we hear very little about this. Yet one thing is certain: the area that is likely to have the most positive impact in terms of population, wealth creation, and development in Africa is governance. We need strong, effective governance nonprofits making a difference, picking away at regimes on the ground, naming and shaming and forcing governments to modify their corrupt and ineffective local governance structures. Free the people from the burden of poor governance, and people will free themselves for the rest. Think Microcredit; think Muhammad Yunus.

What Yunus shows is that people can free themselves from poverty if we stop stopping them—if we help to remove the barriers that keep them in poverty. This works not just in Asia and Africa but in developed countries, too. Microcredit is on the rise in North America and Europe as a way of helping poor, underprivileged members of depressed communities to work their own way to a better life.

There are no easy answers to the questions we are raising here. In fact, for many of the questions there may be no answers at all. Our hope is that we are putting the questions in a new way, one that will cause us to think and to reassess the impacts of globalization on our lives, on our organizations, and on the decisions that we all make as individuals. It seems a generalization to say that everything is changing; however, that statement is probably much closer to the reality than we think. The flat world and the flat philanthropic world are concepts that we are going to have to deal with. They bring to the fore questions that are very uncomfortable. That challenge us. That challenge our values, our preconceptions, our existing ways of doing things, our habits, our ideas, and our world. That challenge our relationships to those around us, both in our local and in our global communities.

I believe very strongly that we need to do three things in response to these questions:

1. Not be afraid to ask them.
2. Not be afraid of the answers, however scary, uncomfortable, and anxiety-generating they may be.
3. Keep true to our values and be the change we want to see in the world.

Part Two

SURVIVING AND THRIVING

Chapter Four

From Fifties to Fractions

Whether we like it or not, we are all citizens of a world dominated by markets. We are surrounded by the mania of markets and live in a society where money is meaning and where freedom does not always equal happiness.

—Karaoke Capitalism

Surviving in the globalized world is first a question about recognizing what a globalized world is. In the first part of this book, we spent time looking at how the globalized world has developed, and what the implications and the realities of this brave new world are. Now let's address some of the ways that we can use these questions and the flat philanthropic world to help grow our organizations.

In the good old days, when a spade was a spade and not a garden improvement facilitator, things were much simpler. Charities had missions, they had beneficiaries, and they had donors. Mostly, the beneficiaries had a need of some sort that they couldn't pay for or weren't aware of, the donors had money and goodwill, and the charities had the capacity to transform the donors' money into services or activities that met those beneficiaries' needs. This is what I call "Fifties Fundraising," as it reminds me of when life was simple, when products did what they said on the boxes, and when everyone knew their role and got on with it, kind of like in the 1950s.

Then the world pancaked.

Nowadays, charities still have missions, beneficiaries (at least for the most part), and donors (again, for the most part). But that is where the similarities end. Today, beneficiaries may be donors, while donors may be beneficiaries; organizations may be providing government services, while governments may be inciting donors to give through tax breaks; beneficiaries may be totally heterogenic, from different groups, societies, and cultures with differing needs; likewise for donors, who may have totally different motivations according to the need they want to fund your organization to meet; organizations may collaborate and each meet only part of the need; and added to all that, now beneficiaries and donors can be anywhere on the planet.

We have moved from "Fifties Fundraising" to "Fraction Fundraising," where every action, intent, or project has to encompass an ever-increasing number of needs, expectations, challenges, and hopes. Fraction Fundraising is about just that—about having the skills, the talent, the tools, and the knowledge to fraction out each objective in order to ensure that it is not just meeting, but optimizing the needs of every stakeholder involved. And, as we have already seen, those needs and expectations are getting higher and higher as the world gets flatter and flatter.

Fraction Fundraising is also about looking to new places and recognizing that the flat world platform allows fractioning on a global level. Today, our donors and our beneficiaries can literally be anywhere on the planet. And so can we. And that is the challenge of fractioning. How can I, as a fundraiser, possibly run such a complex equation of needs and expectations when the individuals behind them could be anywhere in the world?

In November 2001, just a few days after 9/11, a terrible explosion ripped through the city of Toulouse, in southwest France. Windows blew out on houses for miles around the epicenter of the explosion. The blast could be heard more than 70 miles away. The people of Toulouse had no idea what had hit them. It was not terrorists, but the AZF Chemical plant located in the middle of the city exploding after a chemical leak. Six years later, in early summer 2007, after a mammoth cleaning-up operation, the foundation stone was laid for a brand-new cancer research and treatment center—the Canceropole Toulouse, to be built on the site of the old chemical plant.

The cancer center, brainchild of Philippe Douste-Blazy, the former mayor of the city, is being created with a pot of public money, some leading-edge public-private partnerships, and a huge international fundraising drive. The Fondation InNaBioSante has been created to coordinate and pilot the fundraising efforts, and I have had the pleasure of working with them to do it. But the interesting thing about this Foundation is that it could not have existed 10 years ago. It simply would not have had a mandate, or been able to put the same vision together. So what is this vision? It is a global vision, made possible by local capacity. The vision is a world without cancer, so there's nothing new there. But the Foundation believes that the unique infrastructure of the Canceropole Toulouse stands a real chance of bringing them one giant leap closer. Why? Because the center brings together a hospital, research facilities, and clinics, which means that the scientists working in their labs are going to be just a few doors down from the patients in their beds. This closeness should serve both, helping scientists get closer to the real illness and giving patients access to revolutionary new treatment trials. And it also brings together scientists and doctors from around the world, who will be offered short-term research tenures in the state-of-the-art facilities.

So, this is a global project—curing cancer—that is attracting interest from serious funders around the world, from the United States, the Middle East, Asia, and elsewhere. But it is made possible only through the infrastructure provided in one particular area of France thanks to a chemical plant that blew up.

A local response, turned into a global vision, funded by global money, made possible by local capacity: a totally flat philanthropic world concept.

This idea of local closeness and capacity with international reach is a trend that we have been seeing for a number of years. The desire to get closer to grass roots but at the same time reach for the stars is a twenty-first-century paradox. And it doesn't look like it will go away anytime soon. Belonging to a tribe on a local level is increasingly important. If we feel we don't belong to a tribe, we feel lost. And tribes are small-scale operations. But they all have access to the Internet.

Politically, Europe has been following this trend since the fall of the Berlin Wall. Think Yugoslavia. Think even of the United Kingdom, where devolution has given more power to the Scottish, Welsh, and Northern Irish parliaments and locally elected officials than at any time in recent history. The age-old nation is being slowly replaced by more local, more regional, and more tribal gauges of identity. People increasingly want to belong somewhere close.

But this brings us to another question.

What if that somewhere close were global? What if the distinction between local and global actually no longer existed? What if distance now no longer mattered and everything was global?

One thing is clear—the goalposts are moving. In fact, to be more precise, the goalposts are moving on a playing field that is continually tilting in different directions, and neither phenomenon shows any sign of stopping. Quite the contrary.

So how do we navigate these troubled waters to ensure that the reasons our organizations exist continue to be championed? What do we have to do so that the support we provide to our beneficiaries can continue and increase tomorrow? Where is the road map for the flat philanthropic world?

In short, there are no answers. There is no map. The rulebook hasn't been written. Indeed, even if it had been written, the rules would have changed so many times since that it would be completely useless now.

However, this is not satisfactory. We have to have a go, and try to put our collective heads together and come up with something better than that.

Over the past few years, through my work with non-profits and students of philanthropy around the world, I have asked and discussed these questions with hundreds of people. And, I am thrilled to say, there appears to be some kind of consensus. It is too early to say if this consensus will hold. But it exists. And as a result, it is my privilege to be able to share, in the next few chapters, some of the ideas and strategies of this consensus on how we can live, thrive, and survive in the flat philanthropic world.

Chapter Five

The Four-Step Plan to Flat Philanthropic Success

Step 1: Rationalize

Nonprofit organizations are complicated animals. Whereas companies produce, sell, and manage relationships in an environment where the principal objective is making money, we have to produce, sell, and manage relationships in an environment where the principal objective is *not* making money.

This could at first appear to be simpler, but after analysis we realize that it is much more complex. Why?

Because a company has a certain sway over its suppliers, who provide the material wherewithal for them to realize their product and sell it to their consumers.

As nonprofits we are funded by donors who are paying for a service they are not receiving, which means that we have very little sway over our suppliers (our donors). If a company is not happy with the performance of a supplier, it can change and move to another competitor. If we are not happy with the performance of our donors, we cannot simply move to other donors. We are therefore much more dependent on our suppliers. This means that we have to be extra skillful in building relationships, both with donors and with beneficiaries.

However, many nonprofits are structured not around building relationships, but around fundraising, communications, programs, and often a myriad of other activities—topped off with a fairly heavy management/ administration level.

Bruno David is the chair of a small French association, Noir et Blanc. The charity works to fight sickle-cell anemia in Africa through a mix of research, lobbying, and patient care. This very streamlined organization has few staff members, and much of their activity is focused on the ground in the Democratic Republic of Congo. Early in 2007, Bruno and I had a conversation that was to be one of the most important in my fundraising career. The starting point was that Bruno wanted to begin fundraising for his charity to increase income to meet growing demands for their services in Africa. But it all got interesting when I mentioned that to raise money you often needed to invest, at least at the start, and to build capacity, employ talented staff, and give them the opportunity to develop. Bruno didn't seem interested in this. His argument was that Noir et Blanc did two things better than any other organization on the face of the planet: they identified promising research projects into the disease, and they provided hands-on patient care in difficult-to-reach parts of Africa. This was what they did. And they did it better than anyone else. So, the argument went, why should the organization take its eye off the ball and start trying to do something else that was *not* what it did best? Surely it would make more sense to give that over to someone else.

What Noir et Blanc were saying here was not just unusual; it was positively groundbreaking. They had understood what they did better than anyone else on the face of the planet, and they were going to concentrate all their efforts on this. Fundraising? They weren't experts, so they reckoned that there must be someone out there who knew how to do it better than they did. My job was to find these experts and then build partnerships, or subcontracting deals, or whatever they needed in order to raise money, but which didn't involve distracting them from what they did best.

Bruno had applied efficient, mission-driven, powerful logic to a humanitarian problem. And he had done it by asking a key question:

What is the one thing that we do better than anybody else in the world?

And that is the question for the flat philanthropic world. It is the only one that matters.

In the globalized philanthropic world, you are now competing with organizations from around the world, not just in your region or your country; you are competing with organizations from the other side of the planet. If you work in a university, you are competing with Chinese and Indian universities for the best candidates for your lucrative MBA program. If you are an education charity, you are competing for donors' hearts and minds against organizations that provide education in all sorts of other places.

This competition for hearts, minds, and wallets is fierce. And it is not going to get easier. Not everyone will survive. As donors become more individualistic and are offered more choice, their criteria for choosing causes are going to become more personal and more radical. They are going to exercise their rights to be "demanding dictators."

In a world where there are hundreds or even thousands of organizations on the planet doing roughly the same thing as yours, it is the single most powerful key to your survival and growth. What do you do that makes you different from the others? What is the one thing that really characterizes who you are as an organization? What is the *one* thing that you do better than anyone else, anywhere?

This is the core competency of your organization. It is what you should spend your time doing. McDonald's used to say, "We make hamburgers and we make them well." What can *you* say?

Quite simply put, if you do not know today what your core business and values are, you need to find out. And then you need to concentrate on your core competency.

Often, the reaction to this question is to say: "Well, our organization does three things really well, and we couldn't not do any of them." Okay, that's fine, just as long as you have the resources to fund three core competencies! Is your organization that over-resourced that it can afford to do three things exceptionally well? Really? Because if it is, you are going to have a queue of fundraisers wanting to work for you. I have never encountered a nonprofit organization that was sufficiently resourced to do even one thing as well as it would like, let alone more than one. Our limited financial and human resources simply don't allow it. This means that we have the imperative to concentrate on our core value-added proposition and leave the stuff on the side to other people.

Increasingly, we cannot afford to have several core competencies, because the chances are that someone will end up doing each of them better than we do. So what is yours? What makes your organization tick? What is the one thing you are unbeatable at?

Work it out. It's important.

But it's not the end of the process.

Indeed, this is where it gets difficult. Once you know what you do really, really well, then you have to deal with the other stuff that you do, but don't do as well. Noir et Blanc decided that their core competency was delivering treatment for sick people in Africa and identifying promising research programs to fund. This is what they do. Fundraising, donor management, grant writing, and the like are *not* what they do. They have few skills in those areas, so they actively decided to leave them to others who do them much better than Noir et Blanc does them.

Map your organization's activity. Think about what it spends time and resources doing, and ask yourself whether this is really where the most added value comes from. Work out what you collectively don't have many skills in, and then take that list and identify people or other organizations that could do it for you. Then get rid of it. Outsource it. Partner with another group, company, or nonprofit to deliver it. And then find organizations that are doing badly the thing that you do really well. Go see them and offer to do it better for them. Consolidate along your lines of expertise.

It is a hard reality, but many nonprofit organizations are more self-serving than they should be. Over the years, weak leadership and lack of vision can turn fantastic organizations into groups of people who are more about preserving their charity's identity than really helping the maximum number of beneficiaries. If you feel your organization is one of these, then the time has come to take action—or tomorrow it may be one of the first to disappear.

Take this opportunity to look long and hard at your core competency. Work out what makes you great and what makes a real difference. And then do it more and better. And give the rest to someone else to do. Use the huge possibilities opened up by the flat world platform to collaborate, effectively and horizontally, with individuals and organizations around the world.

This is not just a simple outsourcing exercise, about offloading your data entry to India or getting your telemarketing done in Africa. It is about thinking about why your organization exists—what its mission is—and then facing the reality that you will almost certainly be able to achieve it more quickly, with better results and more beneficiaries served, if you rationalize your organization.

Noir & Blanc is a truly flat world operation. They have identified their core competencies and are pursuing them without becoming distracted. They have realized that in order to grow, they need competence and capital—and they consider themselves to be experts in neither so have subcontracted both.

It may be that what we need are nonprofits specialized in fundraising that provide their services at very low fees for charities that cannot afford traditional commercial prices. These would be organizations that are able to add value by being the people who can take on non-core competencies of other organizations.

I predict that this will be the nonprofit organizational model of tomorrow—adding value through horizontal collaboration at all levels except core competency. It may not surprise you too much to hear that Bruno David of Noir et Blanc used to be a director of the Publicis advertising agency.

Many nonprofits around the world have already begun the rationalization process. For instance, not many organizations have internalized their call centers. Even fewer have internalized their database development capacity. And even fewer still have internalized their data entry. However, these are all outsourcing tasks: things that can be easily digitized and moved to cheaper labor. And as we mentioned earlier, this is not just simply about taking parts of your organization's activity and shipping them out somewhere cheaper, but it is about looking at how you can add value through collaboration. It is a process that must enable you to help more beneficiaries and better serve your donors. This is what Noir et Blanc has done—envisaging its development on a totally globalized platform.

And here is where we need to look to the commercial sector for inspiration.

In my view, airlines do rationalization better than most. Arguably it is because they are in one of the most difficult industries—with growing demand being continually offset by things like 9/11 and rising fuel prices. Whatever the reasons, we can learn from them.

Let's imagine a typical airline journey today. You book a ticket online, with a paperless e-ticket. About 24 hours before flying, you go back online and check in, printing your boarding pass as you do so. If you are on a low-cost airline with no reserved seating, you may even want to purchase preboarding vouchers to allow you to avoid the scrum and get on the plane straightaway. Then you turn up at the airport. If you have no bags, you go straight through security and the first time you see an employee of the airline is when someone scans your printed boarding pass at the gate.

Now let's imagine a typical airline journey 10 years ago. You called the airline, and talked to a human being who looked at availability and reserved your ticket. This ticket was then processed, printed, and sent out by post to you, who, upon receiving it, put it somewhere safe. Then you turned up at the airport and joined a queue to check in, where someone took your paper ticket and turned it into a boarding card. Then you went through security and to the gate.

Now, reading this, chances are you're thinking, "Isn't technology good at making our lives simpler?" And you would be right. But you would especially be right because that is exactly what the airlines want you to believe. They want you to believe that all this technology is making life simpler for you. But actually, what it is doing is allowing the airlines to pass you the buck. In a way, it is almost allowing them to make you an unpaid employee! Today you are doing work that yesterday was done by airline staff. You are searching through a database to find the best ticket for you (previously done by staff on the phone), you are printing your own boarding pass and checking yourself in (previously done by staff at the airport), and you are choosing where to sit—often paying a premium for it (again, previously done by staff at the airport).

You have actually turned yourself from a customer into an asset for the company you are flying with. Yes, it has saved you time, although if the airline had the appropriate number of check-in desks open in the first place you wouldn't need to wait in a queue. Fewer check-in desks, fewer people, lower costs, higher profits. All it takes is a good bit of communication for us to think it is *a good idea!*

The airlines have been very clever with this. They have managed to turn their customers into their employees and by doing this save money. Banks have done it, too, through online banking, and other industries are going that way every day.

This is rationalizing.

And this is exactly the sort of thing that nonprofits should be doing.

Rationalization is not just about finding suppliers or other organizational partners to do our non-core competency work for us. It is also about enlisting individuals—stakeholders and others. When you look at the things your organization is not excellent at, look at who is. It may be that your donors can do some of your work better than you. After all, who can best manage their giving history than the donors themselves? It may even be that your beneficiaries can do some of your work for you, especially if you are involved in service provision.

And then work out how to package it in such a way that it becomes a perceived benefit. We think that printing out our boarding passes before arriving at the airport is a real benefit. Let's get donors thinking like that, too.

Rationalizing is not touchy-feely fundraising. It is hard-nosed economics. It is about getting the best results possible. But if industries like airlines and banks (to name but two) are rationalizing daily, why should we as charities be exempt from trying to be as efficient as possible in our mission delivery? Is it just shareholders who deserve the best return? Or do beneficiaries deserve that, too?

I believe strongly that we have an incredible responsibility to our beneficiaries, to the people, animals, or causes that we are trying to serve. How can we possibly stand around and watch while companies get leaner and more efficient and not think that this would be not just important, but fundamental, for *our* beneficiaries? We owe it to them to do our best. If we understand what we do best—what one thing we do better than anyone else and add most value doing—then we are in a much better position to concentrate our efforts on that. Factor in some high-quality horizontal collaboration and a pinch of donor participation, and watch how your beneficiaries get the full benefit.

Step 2: Become Sexy

Without getting too much into Darwinian theory, there are two elements to his work: the survival of the fittest, and the much less known survival of the sexiest.

In the first he relates how the capacity to change is a fundamental element in the development and the continuation of a species. In the second, he returns to a number of points that he first left out in the cold, and analyzes them by saying that in order to survive and thrive you need to not just be the fittest, but you also need to be able to attract to you the fittest member of the opposite sex. Otherwise your chances of continuing your species are slight.

Therefore, he concludes, those who will thrive and survive the most are likely to be those who are the fittest *and* the sexiest.

In a globalized world, where market forces are pushing us toward more competition for our donor dollars, we cannot afford to be just another number in a long list. If we do that we are doomed to fail. We need to be individual; we need to be different. We need to play not on rationality, but on emotion.

As fundraisers, we know that humans are emotional rather than rational beings. We react to the eyes of the dying African child that stare at us from our TV screens more than we would ever react to an annual report. Our instincts, our emotions, are what bite first. "Fight or flight" is *not* "think, fight, or flight." Our first reaction is programmed. It is emotional. It is human. Then the brain engages and wants us to justify our decisions.

"When surplus and sentiments rule, success becomes a question of courting the customers," say Jonas Ridderstrale and Kjell Nordstrom, professors at the Stockholm Business School. Increasingly this is true for charities. We need to court our donors, attract them, seduce them, build relationships with them, and then keep strengthening the bonds so they want to stay with us. Just as a marriage built on guilt is a bad marriage, so is a donor relationship based on anything other than attraction. We give because we want to. Period. Anything else is just a flash in the pan.

So this means that the flat philanthropic world is putting out a huge challenge to the nonprofit world. Surviving and thriving is going to be about being the fittest, the leanest, and the most efficient. It is not going to be simply a question of rationalizing; it is also going to be a question of growing. And growing requires two things: keeping existing supporters and attracting new ones. And sex sells. It attracts, and as every marriage guidance counselor will tell you, it is essential to keeping the attraction going. The question is, how sexy are you?

The Four-Step Plan to Flat Philanthropic Success

The answer, unfortunately for most of us, is not very.

We cannot all be the Angelina Jolies and Brad Pitts of this world. And our organizations are the same. There are very few truly sexy nongovernmental organizations (NGOs). Médecins sans Frontières is one (maybe it's the French thing); Oxfam is another. Unicef is almost one (unfortunately, the association with the UN cold-showers it a bit, though). Greenpeace is arguably one, as could be Amnesty International. And there are certainly others in your country that you think deserve to make the Sexy Charity Awards. But really, they are few and far between.

What is certain, however, is that tomorrow is going to belong to Brad Pitt nonprofit and Angelina Jolie NGO. If Darwin was right, and perceived opinion kind of leans toward the fact that he was, we need to be efficient, performance-driven, and sexy to thrive in the flat philanthropic world of tomorrow.

So how do we get our organizations to appear sexier? To attract more donors? To become *aspirational* brands? How do we inject a big dose of the three-letter word into our work?

I would like to suggest that there are six things that your organization could be doing, and really should be doing, in order to make itself more attractive and turn itself into the sexy brand that you know you have the potential to be.

Define the Need

Above my desk in my office in Paris is a cut-out model of the fundraising cycle. It is a very simple, four-stage cycle: need, audience, technique, evaluation. I look at it regularly, several times a day. And it reminds me of two things: to keep things simple and to do them in the right order. The reason *why* we need money comes before *who* we are going to ask for it, which in turn comes before *how* we are going to ask for it.

It will never, ever be repeated often enough: mission, vision, and values are the fundamental building blocks in every organization. Working out who you are, what you do, and how you do it is the most elemental part of fundraising. But it is also, in my experience, the most neglected.

The Four-Step Plan to Flat Philanthropic Success

There are very few fundraisers who could reply to the question "Why do you need $1,000 now?" with a powerful enough answer to inspire donors to open their wallets. We all have stories of board members who struggle to explain what their organizations do, but often we as fundraisers are not much better.

This has been one of my pet subjects for a while, and over the course of a few workshops at conferences around the world, I began asking participants why, if I were a donor, they really needed my money. Not just really, but really, really, really needed my money. What was the core, fundamental reason that they needed money now? What, at the heart of their organization, was so absolutely essential, fundamental, urgent, and critical that they needed me to immediately, now, straightaway, get out my checkbook and make a donation?

Understandably, when I challenged an individual in a group of his or her own peers with such a simple, yet far-reaching question, the result, more often than not was a total deer-caught-in-the-headlights moment. So in a kindly, group-dynamic-preservation way, I would insist and keep asking the question. The first answer I received would usually resemble in some way the mission statement of the organization—again, more often than not, a dry, institutional phrase designed to appeal to all. So again, in a slightly less kindly way, I would insist. The tension at this point would often be palpable, with everyone else staring actively at the floor in case I decided to pick on them next. And eventually, the fundraiser who was being cross-examined in front of his or her peers would crack, get quite angry, and give me an answer that would blow all the others out of the water.

And systematically, that would happen the fourth time I asked the question.

Let me introduce you to a concept I have called "four times why," and the reason behind it, as confirmed by neurolinguistic programmers and management consultants.

The brain is built in such a way that information is stored in various compartments. The first time we try to access something, we get a very generalized description, and as we move through the *why* process, we start to access different parts of the brain. In short, we move from the general and rational part of the brain to the emotional and irrational part. And we know which of the two is more likely to put a potential donor in touch with his or her checkbook. It usually takes four steps to get here. Sometimes more (hence the "Five why's" that is cited in some management textbooks), but rarely less.

"Four times why" is just a tool—but it does help us access the level of emotional intelligence that our donors are expecting. It helps us move out of our usual way of dealing with information to be able to present it better to others. And because communication is not about what you say, but rather about what your audience hears, this is a very important exercise. Try it, ideally in teams of three. One person asks the question, one person replies, and one person writes down the replies. Try it once and alternate. Then read what you have said. I guarantee it will be more powerful than your current communication, because it will come from the heart. And fundraising communication is designed to go to the heart. QED.

Using "four times why" can be a way of helping a team get focused on a vision, and can even be the starting point of a case for support. However, it is only one part of the process that you and your organization need to go through regularly—every six to 12 months, ideally—to sharpen and redefine your mission, vision, values, and case for support.*

The sharpening aims to do just that—cut out the waffle and get down to the essential. Aim for fewer than 10 words, if possible—memorable, simple words that mean something.

Here are two fantastic mission statements. They are both short, punchy, sexy, and terribly memorable.

1. "Solve unsolved problems innovatively"—3M, the inventor of the Post-it note and countless other things.
2. "Make people happy"—Disney, the purveyor of all things happy, everywhere (except perhaps in Disneyland Paris!).

Without any doubt, the first step to becoming a more sexy organization is to start at the beginning—with

_____

*This is a book that talks about globalization and how to deal with it, so I am assuming that every organization reading this will have those tools in place. If this is not the case, I strongly recommend reading Tom Ahern's excellent new book on cases, *Seeing Through a Donor's Eyes,* to be Published by Emerson & Church in early 2009, a fantastic reference point on the subject.

the need. Make it short. Make it snappy. Make it powerful. And above all, make it emotional and passionate.

Define the Audience and Their Motivations

Humans have a basic need to be recognized and understood. . . . We don't market by saying, "Hello, let me tell you about myself." We market by listening to that person's thoughts and wants and proving our relevance to that perspective and those desires.

—Katya Andressen, *Robin Hood Marketing*

As in many AIDS-afflicted countries, encouraging the use of condoms was not a simple affair in Cambodia. Typically, in such situations, it is more often than not the men who are the problem, and here this was also the case. Campaigns were being run regularly, by both the government and NGOs, but they invariably focused on the long-term impact of not wearing a condom. The problem was that this gave men the opportunity to reply, "AIDS may kill me in 10 years' time, but I may step on a land mine tomorrow. I can't worry about things so far in the future."

Population Services International, an NGO that works around the world on such issues, understood this very masculine reaction, and understood what it was masking—cultural hesitation about condom use. So the NGO changed tack, and positioned themselves as a brand. They brought out a new range of condoms called Number 1 and heavily marketed them as the ideal virility tool. A man without Number 1 was simply not a man. Since the launch of Number 1 in 1994, hundreds of millions have been sold.

This campaign worked because it understood very precisely and very directly the motivations and aspirations of the target audience. The first campaign worked closely with the target market during development and through rollout to ensure that the messages were absolutely spot-on. The NGO understood, no doubt through some good psychological or behavioral analysis—or maybe just by talking to Cambodian women—what the real, hidden motivations of the audience were.

In the flat philanthropic world, we all have multiple audiences. And they are segmenting to finer and finer levels on an almost a daily basis. We saw earlier how geography is being replaced by biography. This is causing our campaign audiences to expect different things from our organization. And I am sure that I will shock no one by asserting that nonprofits are globally relatively unsophisticated in audience analysis and profiling. In order to be a sexy organization tomorrow, we must invest more today in research and analysis, and above all we must test. Many proponents of focus groups will encourage you to run such groups and ask people what they think. They suggest that you get a group of target audience demographics in a room, show them your campaign, and ask them what they think of it.

This is all well and good for a poster campaign. But for fundraising, you can forget it. The only way to tell if a fundraising message will work is to test it. Why? Because donors lie in focus groups. It's as simple as that. They are fantastic at telling you, on an intellectual or abstract level, which of your three test mail packs would be the most likely to elicit a positive response from them. But between intellectual, abstract thinking and donor realities there is a huge chasm, and donors tend to be very good at underestimating its depth. What we think will raise money often doesn't, and vice versa.

This is where we enter into the deep and terribly psychological world of the so-called donation equation, or the act of moving someone to make a donation. There is no absolute reference work on this subject. Indeed, there are arguably as many reasons and ways to get people to make donations as there are people. However, there is one key that we can rely on at all times—heart, head, wallet. Start with the emotion; then back it up with credibility, trust, and confidence; then make the ask.

So, let's work out who we want to talk to. And then let's test how best we can talk to them. And who said fundraising was not a science?!

Here are, thanks to Katya Andressen, some key questions to ask when thinking about audiences, which will help in the identification process:

- What demographic, geographic, and biographic groups do they belong to?
- What do they most care about? What are the most important issues and problems in their lives? What concerns keep them awake at night?
- Have they ever taken the action we're seeking? What happened? If they have not taken that action, what do they do instead?

- What or who constitutes our competition? What messages have they been sending out?
- What appeals to them about our action, and what do they see as easy or hard about it? How close are they to taking action?
- Who approves or disapproves of their taking action? Who influences them? Do other people around them take our action?

As the philanthropic world gets flatter, donors are going to come from everywhere—and nowhere—and demand to be treated as individuals. This means understanding today who your donors are and what their expectations are, and dialoguing with them. This also means testing, testing, and testing some more.

Tell a Story

Stories are how we remember things. Stories translate information into emotion. Bullet points and lists are forgotten the moment we hear them, but we remember stories and anecdotes. Our ancestors communicated the values and the intellectual capital of their tribes by telling stories. Some argue that many religious texts are great stories designed to pass on content. Kids love stories and remember them (I'm sure we can all remember one story we loved to hear as a child). Stories are the future!

Define a Chief Storytelling Officer (CSO), whose job it is to turn your activity into stories that people will remember.

While you're at it, define a Donor Experience Officer (DEO), whose job it is to map and understand the donors' experience at all stages of their relationship with you.

Step 3:
Use Your Body

Back in 1971, Dr. Albert Mehrabian published what was to become one of the most widely quoted (and misquoted) pieces of communication theory. Known as the 7%–38%–55% Rule, it analyzes how people decide whether they like other people. That's pretty important stuff for fundraisers!

The 7%–38%–55% Rule refers to three different parts of communication—verbal and nonverbal—identified by

Dr. Mehrabian: words, tone of voice, and body language, in that order.

In essence, what this tells us is that we get more of a *feeling* about someone from how they act and how they say things than from what they actually say. And it makes sense when you think about it. Let's say you see some people you don't know at a friend's party. Chances are you will probably have a pretty good idea of whether you want to talk to them from observing them across the room. You will interpret their reactions, their facial expressions, the way they stand or sit in relation to anyone they are talking to—this and much more, at a subconscious level. And all this will form your general impression of them. The person sitting on his or her own with legs and arms crossed away from everyone else is not sending out "come talk to me" signals, even if he or she may be an incredibly interesting person.

What I find challenging as a fundraiser is how we use this information. And let's be honest; most of us don't use it enough, if at all. Above and beyond the obvious implications of Dr. Mehrabian's work (and that of Richard Bandler and other neurolinguistic programmers) for how fundraisers use their body language and nonverbal communication skills to build rapport with donors, we have the opportunity to learn a great deal from some of the principles here.

First, when we communicate are we using enough nonverbal cues? Not just in our face-to-face communications, but also in our written, designed, offline, or online communications? Do we look at our brochures, our web sites, our Direct Response Television advertisements through this same verbal/nonverbal filter? Dr. Mehrabian is quick to point out that his research and findings should not be applied to anything but individuals communicating about feelings and likes/dislikes. But the principles still apply. The idea that you get a feeling from each piece of communication that you receive still holds true, regardless of whether it respects the 7%-38%-55% Rule.

This feeling is fundamental to how you integrate the message that the communication is sending you. In fact, it is so fundamental that Marshall McLuhan may just have been right when he said in 1964 that "the medium is the message." The medium is the feeling—the impression that you get, at a subconscious level, before you have a chance to read the print. You don't believe me? Here is a neat little exercise to try it.

The Four-Step Plan to Flat Philanthropic Success

The Distance Test

Set up your computer over the other side of the room—just near enough so that you can see the screen but far enough away that you won't be able to read the text that appears on it. Ask two friends or colleagues to select a dozen or so web sites from different sectors (profit, non-profit . . . maybe including your organization's own site). Then one friend gets behind the terminal and starts going through the sites, while the other grabs a pen and paper to note down what you say. You, from the other side of the room, call out the general impression that you get from each site, what it makes you feel or think of—whatever spontaneously comes to mind.

When you are done, come together and go back through the sites comparing your initial impressions with the real content of the sites. It often makes for pretty interesting learning.

The organizations that are going to thrive and survive in the flat philanthropic world will be those that have understood that being sexy is about sending out the right messages—the messages that say, "Come talk to me. I'm really interesting and exciting and you would love to be associated with me!"—the messages that prove that you are not the bore in the corner but the lively guy or girl whom everyone wants to be like.

Body language as a basis for fundraising communications? Is that really possible? It is, but only if we stop considering that the most important thing is not what we have to say but how we say it. Have a look at the two web sites at www.amnesty.fr and www.oxfam.org.uk. Which one is more inviting? If they were people, which one would you want to talk to? The one with big colorful photos and reader-friendly text? Or the one that is densely packed with oh-so-important information, the one that seems to feel that it is essential to tell us absolutely as much as possible and cram as much stuff as possible into the shortest possible space and time?

Again, think about this for a moment. Who do we like talking to? People who ask questions, who seem interested in us, who share some provocative thoughts? Or people who, as soon as they've got your attention, cram as much information as possible into you in the shortest possible time?

I think it may well have been the great fundraising mentor Ken Burnett who said, "Never forget how unimportant you are in the lives of your donors." This may just be a seminal quote! Why? Well, not-for-profits around the world are populated by really passionate people. Whether you are fighting climate change, or fighting to change mentalities and behaviors, or fighting to save lives in Africa, or fighting for better policy and freedoms for civil society . . . whatever it is you do, the chances are you are pretty passionate about what you are fighting for; otherwise you'd be off making much more money doing something else somewhere else. And the chances are that most of the people in your organization are pretty passionate, too. Because what you are doing is important. In fact, it is so important that many of the people you work with simply can't understand why it is taking so long to make real change. Many of your colleagues or volunteers think that this is really obvious stuff, that solutions already exist and we have the tools to make the world of tomorrow a much better place—so why aren't we doing it? We all know what we should be doing, after all! They are passionate. You are passionate. And you are fighting for a cause that is so important. Come on, guys, let's make this happen now!

The line between passion and preaching is a fine one. And to be honest, I have met many a fundraiser who hasn't known how to avoid crossing it—people who I wish would just stop shouting about their cause. Just because they believe it passionately doesn't mean that everybody else in the world has the same level of commitment. I would love to be able to support work on climate change, but if that means receiving e-mails about how the world is going down the drain, then I don't think I can cope with that over breakfast. I'd rather receive a couple of photos of really pretty places that had been preserved thanks to the help of people like me. That would be nicer.

We all have different levels of commitment to causes. But the vast, vast majority of donors are never going to be as committed as we are. And we need to recognize that. Currently, so many of our organizations are the party equivalent of the person who collars you in the kitchen and never stops talking—the sort of person you need an excuse to get away from. A few, such as Oxfam, have managed the transition. I'd want to talk to an Oxfam person at a party. They look like fun, and I'm pretty sure we'd have a good chat, and maybe a bit of a laugh. I'm fairly sure they wouldn't start to cram oh-so-important information down my throat as soon as we were introduced.

Step 4: Get Hypersensitive (Thanks to Brian the Branding Snail)

Much of the content in this book would merit many more books to explore in more detail. And no more so is this the case than with the concept of hypersensitivity.

Let's return to the friend's party for a while. We've talked about the *feeling* that you get on a subconscious level from the body language of different people and how you often know what they are like even without talking to them. Well, this is the *before* part of the equation. What about the *after* part? What do you take away from an exchange or a conversation with someone at a party? Chances are you take away some of your first impression, especially if it has been confirmed, with a lot of added stuff that you gleaned from the conversation (verbal and nonverbal) and from the way it ended and you moved off to talk to someone else.

To make a slightly strange transition, now I want you to imagine a snail. Call the snail Brian, just for fun.

As Brian moves across the ground, in his slow and steady fashion, he leaves a trace behind him. You can see where he's been. If Brian tells you that he has not been munching on the leaves of your potted plant, you only have to look at the traces on the ground to show whether he's telling the truth or not.

Now, Brian has a distinct advantage over us humans. His trace remains visible. We can see where he has been and what he's been up to (we are Brian's Big Brother?!). Why is this an advantage? Because we all leave a trace. Whoever we are, wherever we go, whatever type of organization we are, we all leave a trace behind us as we interact with people and our surroundings. The difference is that ours is invisible. In fact, it is more than just invisible; it is a closely guarded secret.

This is why Brian is at an advantage. His trace is visible, so it can be analyzed and improved. The traces that nonprofit organizations leave behind in the hearts and the minds of their stakeholders are much more difficult to see, and hundreds of times more difficult to analyze.

But, they are fundamental. Just in the same way as the *feeling* you have before meeting someone is going to play a huge part in whether you want to interact with them or not, the *trace* that you are left with will be the biggest determining factor as to whether you want to interact with them again.

Today's trace is the controlling factor in what happens tomorrow. It is the future. And for fundraisers, it is the unsaid, often unanalyzed trace that will largely influence the behavior of donors in the future.

A trace is much more than just a feeling. In fact, I would argue that your trace is your brand. It is nothing less than the most important asset that your organization has. Your trace is up there with a database or an endowment. It is one of the key founding elements of your organization and one of the key determining elements in its success and growth tomorrow.

Think back to the last organization you gave money to. Go back through your own donation process. Why did you decide on this cause? Maybe it is an organization you have been giving to for a while, or maybe it was the first time. What happened—did you respond to a mailing or to a phone call, or was

it a face-to-face meeting? Think back to that moment
when you made out the check—what were you feeling? Hope, excitement, elation, a deep conviction that
this was the right thing to be doing? Now keep thinking . . . follow the process through. Did you receive a
thank-you? Did you get thanked quickly? Did it meet
your expectations? Honestly, now. Did the way the
charity acknowledge your gift meet the expectation
that you had when you made the gift? Did you end up
feeling that this organization was just the greatest in
the world? Were your feelings of hope, excitement, or
elation fulfilled? Or were you left feeling that actually
you were probably just one in a long list of other people and that you didn't really matter that much, and
your donation probably didn't really mean that much
to the organization? Now think about your future
giving intentions. Are you planning to give to that
organization again or not? Are you planning to give
more? Were you so moved and impressed by the whole
experience that you will be giving twice as much next
time and recommending them to friends, or were you
left feeling that it was probably a good idea to support them, but that you're not going to go down to

the ATM and withdraw your life savings tomorrow to give them?

Your trace as an organization is what is left when everything else is gone—what is left when your interactions with a particular donor have happened and you both have moved on, either temporarily or permanently, to other things.

It is not just about the thanking process, although Penelope Burk in her fantastic book *Thanks!* (Burk & Associates Ltd, 2000) shows just how important this is—a frighteningly high percentage of donors admit to giving less the first time to see how a charity is going to react. It is about the trace you leave in the hearts and minds of the donor when he or she has moved on. That trace is what they remember of you. What they think of you. What they are going to tell other people about you. Once again, it is, to all extents and purposes, your brand.

So how do you influence a trace? Is it possible to change the trace you leave in your donors' hearts and minds?

I believe that it is.

But to do so requires a fairly extensive overhaul of an organizational culture, so you've got to want to do it. Indeed, it may be too much work for many nonprofits to undertake. It requires leadership and vision as well as time and rigor. But I am convinced that the organizations that are going to thrive in the flat philanthropic world will do it. Indeed, many I have spoken to recently are aware of the implications and have already started, in one sense or another, to work toward it. Where do you fit in?

Concretely, how do we go about it?

An organization's trace is determined by its interactions with its audiences. It is almost a sum total of all of the interactions. So the first stage to decrypting it is to begin to understand the interactions.

Interaction mapping is about listing all of the possible interactions that a donor can have with your organization. This can start with a call center or a reception desk, but goes way further. We need to think about physical and virtual interactions with all aspects of the organization.

The physical could therefore start with the reception desk, but will also include the physical aspect of staff that are at the reception desk, in fact all staff that a donor may meet. It will also include the physical state of the reception area itself or of the building—is it warm and friendly or cold and antiseptic, like a doctor's waiting room? Did the donor have to go up a dimly lit set of stairs to get to your office?

It will then go on to include all aspects of your written communication—brochures, mailings, the logo, the typefaces used, the photos. What is the general impression (think back to the discussion of body language) that you are leaving?

Next is the interaction process itself—the thanking process, the welcome process, and each of the physical communication objects (letters, etc.) used.

And so on.

Then on a virtual level, what are people saying about you? What has the press said about you recently? What is your understanding of the perception that the public has of you—are you a sexy, dynamic organization that people want to be associated with, or again, are you the organizational equivalent of the boring guy who talks *at* you at parties and whom you can't get away from?

What does your staff say when called up on the phone? Or what impression does your telemarketing team give?

This mapping process is comprehensive. It is designed to be. It has to be to give you the full picture of all of the interactions with your organization. And it is the first stage of the process.

The second stage of the process is much more difficult and involves a certain amount of honesty. Here we start to build the "Trace/Touchpoint Matrix."

Trace/Touchpoint Matrix

Touchpoint	Current trace—what people think today	Ideal trace—what you would like people to think tomorrow
Mailings	Indifferent, too forceful, looks like last month's pack	Engaging, with powerful stories—*I want to open it*
Outgoing calls	Unfriendly, cold and pressuring	Warm, friendly, passionate—*I feel great after receiving call*
Face to face (street) fundraisers	Shabby, bored	Energetic and dynamic—*I am proud to be a part of their cause*
Offices/shops	Old, not welcoming	Warm, comfortable, homely—*I could pop in if I was passing*

160

Web site	Difficult to navigate, too complicated	Simple, effective and engaging—*I find what I am looking for and go back regularly*
E-mail newsletter	Full of text and comes too often – don't read it	Colorful, positive, different—*I look forward to it*
Helplines	Only call when I have to – long waits and pressured staff/volunteers	Warm, calm, and open—*they really have the time to listen and understand my needs*
Information points . . .	Not maintained, always a bit shabby	Full of interesting documentation—*I take things home for my family and friends*

etc. . . .

For each interaction, or touchpoint, that you have identified in the mapping process, we now need to attribute an ideal value—what we would like the interaction to feel or look like.

For example, when a donor telephones your organization, you would probably like the response to be warm, friendly, helpful, and efficient. In that case, this would be your ideal value for that interaction or touchpoint.

In the case of your mail packs, you would maybe like the ideal value to be dynamic, human, emotional, and engaging. This then gets noted down in the matrix.

The third stage of the process is where a large dose of honesty comes in. Having defined the ideal value for each of the touchpoints, it is time to define the real value. What is the current reaction to each of the interactions you have listed? How do your donors (or non-donors) really react to your logo, or to your web site, or to your latest publication? Are they having the desired impact (your ideal value) or are they off the mark?

In my experience, it is better to avoid running formalized focus groups to get this kind of information. Get a friend whom you trust to call your receptionist a couple of times, and go down into the subway and ask people about your logo or mail pack. Ask people walking past your building what they think of it. Speak to a couple of donors you know well and ask them to tell you honestly how you compare with other organizations they give to (it is always more helpful to ask for a comparison as a starting point rather than asking point-blank how people feel, as most will give a stock answer that everything is fine, especially if you are in the UK!).

Be honest—frightfully, horribly honest. Try to get as close to the reality of your audiences' perceptions as you can. And remember that you will gain nothing from kidding yourself that you are better than you really are.

This may well have been the first time that you have gone through this kind of process—that you have sat down and asked yourself what the ideal, desired reaction to your mail packs or your logo or your receptionist is and how it compares with the current reaction. Be aware that simply by doing this, you will be changing things for the better. You will be gaining an increased understanding of what you are actually trying to achieve and how close to the mark you are. So even if the next stage of the process seems like somewhat of a challenge, be assured that you are already on the scoreboard and moving in the right direction, because you now have this understanding.

But don't let that be an excuse for not moving to the final stage of the process, change—or more precisely, moving from real to ideal.

Select two' or three areas of your Trace/Touchpoint Matrix. They could be areas where the delta between the ideal and the real is greatest. Or they could be the most strategic areas for your fundraising. Whichever you choose, do not take more than three at a time.

The aim here is to start implementing changes and processes that will help you move from the real to the ideal trace value. Change is difficult in any organization, and change management is an increasing part of any development director's job. To help in this process, I would like to recommend a tool that was developed by David Gleicher in the '60s and that has been adapted by countless consultants since: the Change Equation.* Our sister company, The Imaginist Company, uses a version of the change equation with clients in the UK.

The principle is that real, positive change will happen only in an organization when there are sufficiently strong factors to overcome the resistance which is there in any organization. The resistance is a mixture of inertia, fear, and the effort needed to make the change and can be expressed as the Cost of Change.

---

*Beckhard, R. and David Gleicher, 1969. *Organization Development: Strategies and Models.* Reading, MA: Addison-Wesley.

Gleicher discovered that only a combination of a powerful Vision, a clear way forward ("Next steps") and Dissatisfaction with the status quo was sufficient to overcome the cost of change.

This gives us the change equation—a simple algebraic formula to help achieve long-lasting change.

Vision $\times$ Next steps $\times$ Dissatisfaction $>$ Cost of Change

Vision

Perhaps the simplest element of the equation is vision. You need to have the dream that change is a good idea. You need to show people the top of the mountain, get them excited about being at the top, and help them see what things will look like once the change has happened.

Next Steps

To continue with the mountain metaphor, it is easy to get people convinced that the top of the mountain is a sexy and exciting place to be, but if they see only the mountain, it looks like an impossible and unachievable task. So you need to break down the ascension of the summit into scalable and achievable packages, the first of which can be implemented simply just by doing X or Y. It really is about showing people which direction they need to move off in when they start.

Dissatisfaction

But by far the most difficult part of change, and the one that is the most neglected, is the notion of dissatisfaction. People are naturally conservative. Their feet are naturally stuck to the ground. The status quo and the comfort zone of here and now are very powerful and very effective at gluing people's feet to the ground. Basic physics tells us that it will always take more energy to get an object moving from a stationary state than to accelerate the movement once it is ongoing. And change is subject to basic physics. So you need to find a way of unsticking people's feet from the ground.

And, unsavory as it may sound, the most effective way of doing this is to generate dissatisfaction. Make them realize that the ground they are standing on is unstable, sinking, about to be hit by lightning, in an earthquake zone, or in the path of an oncoming fast-moving and heavy object. In short, make them realize that the cost of not changing is shortly going to be greater than the cost of changing, that they are soon going to be in danger if they don't change, and that the result will be *way* more uncomfortable than starting to move now.

This may involve asking some fairly searching questions, such as:

Is the current situation meeting all of our hopes?

Are we as good as we could be?

What is missing at the moment that is preventing us from being better than we are today?

What might improve the current situation?

And finishing off with:

Can I share with you some ideas on how we might achieve that?

Creating dissatisfaction is a key part of ensuring change. It also has the advantage of empowering other decision makers, staff, or volunteers to believe that the decision to change was theirs!

So, to return to the Trace/Touchpoint Matrix and the three key areas you have decided to work on, take the change equation tool and apply it.

What is the vision for each area? What would it mean to be able to achieve the ideal that you set out in the matrix for this area? What would it mean, for example, if all donors felt that each phone interaction with your organization was warm, friendly, helpful, and efficient? What sort of difference would that make for the donors, but more importantly (for the people you are trying to get to change) for the organization and for them?

What would happen if you, as an organization, decided not to make this change? What would be the cost, both to your fundraising and to your capacity to meet the needs of your beneficiaries in a fast-moving world where other organizations are starting to realize the importance of this kind of thinking and are integrating donor satisfaction (donor delight?) as fundamental concepts in their donor relationship management?

And what do you need to do next? What are the tangible next steps that you have to take to make the move from real to ideal? They can be small steps, in the Japanese style of *kaizen*—"constant improvement." There is no need to make people fearful of a big quantum jump. That can come later once they are on board.

Your trace is your brand. It is one of your most powerful assets as an organization. And it is up to the fundraiser to work out what it is, to quantify it, to qualify it, and to make the changes that your donors are hoping for. In this way, your organization can have the tools to thrive in the world of tomorrow—by setting clear objectives, getting out there, and making the difference!

Interestingly, while talking about change and engaging donors, the *Harvard Business Review* published in August 2002 a paper linking the strength of community and innovation. The paper found that the stronger the community, the less it innovated and grew economically. And the less the community was linked and tied together, the more it innovated and grew economically. What does this tell us?

- Established communities tend to have routines and behavior patterns that normalize and discourage people who do not fit in.
- Less established communities, where keeping up with the Joneses is less important, are the ones where individuals feel freer to innovate and to develop new ideas.

Think of your organization as a community. Which type would it be? A closely knit environment that doesn't encourage people to be different, or an open environment that accepts and welcomes all types of people and encourages them to play to their strengths and to develop new ideas? If you fall into the first category, you'd probably better have a chat with your human resources person, because as a fundraiser you are going to be in trouble.

To succeed, we need more, not fewer nonconformists.

Chapter Six

Balancing Out the Future Fundraising Mix

Surviving and thriving is about being sexy, about defining the ultimate donor experience, about being aspirational. But more than anything it is about knowing where to turn for support.

Lester Salamon's *Global Civil Society Review,* published by John Hopkins University, tells us that, on a global level, the vast majority (upwards of 80 percent in some countries) of philanthropic income comes from individuals. Then come corporates, groups, foundations, and other sources, often with less than 10 percent each.

Will this balance stay the same while globalization and the flat philanthropic world shift boundaries and playing fields around asking, giving, and receiving?

The way money comes into organizations today is almost always in direct correlation with the way the society operates. In a country like France, for example, where the state has traditionally been very strong, the vast majority of funding (up to 100 percent in certain sectors such as health care and parts of education) comes from the public sector. In a country like the United States, where community-based philanthropy has traditionally been fundamental in public service provision, it is not surprising that we find higher levels of individual engagement with philanthropy. So as societies change, what does this mean for fundraising? In France the government recently changed a law that had prevented public universities from raising private funds. As a result many of these institutions have, more or less overnight, moved into active fundraising, targeting companies first and then moving on to individuals.

Let's look therefore at individuals, grant makers, corporations, and governments and see what effect globalization is having on their philanthropy.

Giving According to Whose Needs?

Cast your mind back to December 2004, just after Christmas—the 26th, to be precise. Maybe you were doing something similar to what I was doing—sitting on the sofa at home, full after a veritable orgy of food and wallowing in the overconsumption that the festival of Christmas has become.

In fact, I was in front of the TV when it happened, watching repeats of old shows and films. The ultimate comfort zone, some would say. Full, contented, warm, laughing at things I had laughed at many times before. I think I may even have been wearing slippers.

And then the story broke. "We are getting reports of an earthquake in Southeast Asia . . . of a tsunami. . . ." As the news unfurled, the horror of this catastrophe started to become clear. The images started to filter through. The rolling news services did their job, using the full power of the flat world platform—searching out and finding amateur images from the event, and then putting them on high rotation, feeding them into the collective psyche. Media around the world ran images that many of us will never forget—of the destruction, the chaos, but more than anything of that wave coming in and obliterating everything in its path.

Over the next few days, the world witnessed a philanthropic mobilization without precedent—one that would simply dwarf responses to Ethiopian famine, Darfur, and every other major international catastrophe. On January 26, one month after the event, the *Chronicle of Philanthropy* reported that "the International Federation of Red Cross and Red Crescent Societies, together with its network of more than 180 national societies, had raised $1.2-billion, which the organization says will be sufficient to pay for its relief efforts. The Federation noted that 85 percent of the money raised had been donated or pledged by individuals." Total U.S. giving at this time was estimated at $597 million, way in excess of the U.S. governmental pledge of just $350 million. These were serious amounts of cash.

The wave hit on December 26th. Fundraising started almost immediately. Well, actually, no, it didn't. Donations started pouring in almost immediately, but organized fundraising didn't start until the 28th or the 29th—most directors of fundraising were on holiday. In the United Kingdom, the Disasters Emergency Committee (a fantastic organization that brings together the leading overseas aid charities to fundraise together at times of major crisis) didn't launch until the 29th.

But just because we took a couple of days to get our campaigns up and running didn't mean that the public waited. Quite the contrary. Indeed, the collective outpouring of philanthropic grief started almost immediately—triggered by the images and the shocking nature of the catastrophe. And between the 25th and the 29th, charity web sites around the world crashed one after another because of the incredible number of donations that were coming through.

The first coordinated asks started hitting just before the New Year. Special fundraising telethons, company collections, street collections, you name it—all over the world, in both developed and developing countries, individuals were putting their hands in their pockets and digging deep.

Then, on the 5th of January, out of nowhere, Doctors Without Borders went public telling donors that they had enough money for the emergency relief on the ground after the tsunami.

As Catrin Schulte-Hillen, U.S. program director of Médecins sans Frontières (MSF), noted at the time in an interview on the web site Democracy Now!, "We also want... to underline that while the tsunami disaster has traumatized people in all of those countries and has traumatized us . . . we cannot forget that there [are] other conflicts and other crises in this world, which sometimes we don't get to see."

This is the crunch.

Médecins sans Frontières, although they caused a huge uproar from the nongovernmental organization (NGO) sector at the time, was right. But that really isn't the issue. Whether MSF was right or wrong, or whether they managed the communication around the announcement in an optimum way or not, is beside the point.

Because the point is that there *were* other conflicts and other crises in the world, as there still are, which we weren't getting to see. The tsunami was an incredible catastrophe, with more than 250,000 losing their lives. But it was not the only catastrophe at the time, or since. Think Darfur, or the 5.4 million people killed in the last ten years of civil war in the Congo.

So why was the world getting into all sorts of philanthropic outpourings over the tsunami, and not over other crises? Well, there are hundreds of reasons why the tsunami galvanized public opinion and sympathy in the way it did, and much has been written about this subject since the event. My aim here is not to try to add to this opus, but to highlight what I think probably the key reason. Simply put, I think it was because we had never seen a tsunami before. In fact, more to the point, we had never had amateur video of a tsunami destroying everything and everyone in its path beamed into our living rooms via rolling news media. It was new. It was powerful. And it was shocking.

I know that I went online to the Red Cross web site within minutes of seeing the first images of the wave on TV. And I know from asking friends and colleagues that I was not alone in doing this. Why did I react this way? Simply because it was the only thing I could possibly do to feel less helpless in the face of such an incredible force of destruction.

We all know that philanthropic outpourings are not directly correlated to destruction, death, or suffering, but to a number of factors or variables. We have images on our TV screens of starving African children. There is no longer anything new there. It was new in

1984 when the BBC journalist Michael Buerk broke the story of the Ethiopian famine and sent these images into our living rooms for the first time. And it got a reaction then—Band Aid, Live Aid, and others.

But let's return to the tsunami and to MSF for a minute. Essentially, MSF was saying, just a week after the wave hit, that donors should stop giving to MSF. So did they? Did donors stop giving to MSF? Of course not. They kept on giving.

Why?

The answer, unfortunately, is very simple. Individuals did not give according to the needs of the beneficiaries. They gave according to their needs as donors. Otherwise they would have stopped giving when MSF asked them to and they would have given to other crises like Darfur or the Congo instead.

This is a very, very worrying state of affairs. It is, of course, one that has always existed. Every charity has a list of things that it could fundraise for. Some of them are easier to sell than others. The handicapped charity that spends the majority of its money on putting drunk drivers back together after accidents is not going to raise a fortune if they write to their donors asking to finance wheelchairs for drunk drivers. So they run campaigns about poor, handicapped kids.

But the tsunami was the first-ever international catastrophe that occurred in the flat philanthropic world. Ethiopia, Bhopal, and Kosovo had all been pre-flatness.

The flat philanthropic world made it possible for eyewitness images of the crisis to be sent within hours into billions of homes around the world through the Internet, cable TV, and rolling news. A simple video taken from a mobile phone was suddenly beamed across the world.

And the response was overwhelming. Again, remember that the first active fundraising asks made by nonprofits did not hit until the news was at least a day old. And the majority did not reach donors for an additional two or three days. So who was doing the fundraising?

Initially, no one. People were making spontaneous gifts. Enough people to crash web sites. Unprecedented numbers of people.

And then the media became fundraisers. Then companies became fundraisers. Retailers became fundraisers. In fact, more or less anyone became a fundraiser.

And we were not prepared for any of it.

The challenge has been clearly thrown down to us as a profession. The flat philanthropic world has taken the control over fundraising out of our hands. As soon as there is an event—something worthy of media coverage, which tugs on the emotional heartstrings of the general public—we are going to find ourselves increasingly losing control of our fundraising.

And the real challenge is that it doesn't have to be another international catastrophe. A local event, picked up on by local media and about which local people feel strongly, could be enough to influence giving to a cause without fundraisers getting involved. A well-known and respected local firefighter who loses his life could provoke an outpouring of donations to the firefighters' benevolent fund web site without the fundraisers ever having to get involved.

And tomorrow, when the flat world has pushed back the boundaries of technology even further, and we can all make donations instantly from our mobile phones using simple voice-activation technology that then debits our bank account and wires the funds through to the charity of choice, it is going to become even more difficult to keep the control over our fundraising.

The tsunami was the first flat world catastrophe, and it showed us clearly how external forces like the media and public opinion are much stronger than our internal fundraising forces. It also won't be the last. And as technology moves forward we are going to be faced more and more with the same reality—individuals will increasingly give according to their needs and not according to the needs of the beneficiaries.

And let us not forget that more than 80 percent of all privately fundraised resources come from individuals.

This is why we are going to need some serious balancing.

With the economy expanding at an unforeseen speed, personal wealth reaching unimaginable heights, technological innovations making this speed faster and faster, globalization threatening to wipe out the weak economies and the poor people from the economic map, it is time to consider the case of Social Business Entrepreneurs more seriously than we did ever before. Not only is it not necessary to leave the market solely to the personal-gain seekers, it is extremely harmful to mankind as a whole to do that. It is time to move away from the narrow interpretation of capitalism and broaden the concept of market by giving full recognition to Social Business Entrepreneurs . . . to make the market work for social goals as efficiently as it does for personal goals.

—Muhammad Yunus, from the Grameen Bank Web site (www.grameen-info.org/bank/socialbusinessentrepreneurs.htm)

High-Impact Philanthropy

If our individual donors are increasingly able to choose their own causes and their own ways of giving regardless of the real needs of the beneficiaries, we have a real challenge. Recently, I was at a meeting with a number of development directors from major international NGOs discussing what to do about the changing models of philanthropy, as depicted by Kiva, Global Giving, and others. The good old days, when we, the donor, the beneficiary, and the charity had a nice, interdependent relationship, look like they may be coming to an end

182

forever. Donors no longer need charities to decide where to contribute their money. They can go to Kiva and decide precisely what beneficiary they are going to give to. What's more, they can read all about the project in advance, and then receive information from the beneficiary as the project develops following their donation.

Recently I went to the Kiva web site to do a bit of research for this book, and I was met with a page on the web site telling me that Kiva was no longer accepting donations. A charity was no longer accepting donations! Kiva had more donors than it had projects that needed financing!

How many other organizations (with perhaps the exception of MSF after the tsunami!) can you think of that put up a web page saying they don't need any more money? I can't think of many, if any.

Why is Kiva such a success? Why is Global Giving growing so quickly? Because donors feel empowered, feel close to the beneficiaries, and feel that they can actually make a difference. And in addition, with Kiva, the money is invested into a loan that is then repaid, which means that you can reattribute your funds many times—thereby multiplying the impact of your initial donation.

New economic models are changing the face of philanthropy. I put the Kivas and Global Givings of this world into a category that I call "high-impact philanthropy."

It is definitely a trend, and in much the same way as globalization can be argued about forever, it *is*. High-impact philanthropy now exists. And it is calling organizations to change their thinking and, to a certain extent, their business models.

To return to our meeting with the development directors, the key question to come out of the discussion was that large international NGOs have a challenge ahead. They need to define their added-value proposition to donors in a much clearer and more powerful way than in the past. Brand will always be important, and as we saw after the tsunami, it was the leading nonprofit organization brands (the Red Cross at the top of the list) that picked up most of the money. But the Kivas of this world have shown that brand is not everything and that new operations in niche markets can quickly emerge and position themselves as challengers.

What is it about Save the Children or Oxfam that makes them more appropriate and effective as destinations for philanthropy than being able to give directly to the beneficiary? What is it that means that these organizations can also claim to be players in the high-impact philanthropy market? These are questions that have yet to be answered, but will be essential in the development of these big organizations in the flat philanthropic world. After all, we have all seen how, in the airline market, Easyjet and Southwest came from nowhere to challenge the existing carriers. (And we also know who is winning that particular battle.) If someone can give me a good reason why the philanthropic market shouldn't follow the same trends, I'd be thrilled to hear it.

Capital for Good

Muhammad Yunus received the Nobel Peace Prize in 2007 for his work in promoting and developing microcredit and social enterprise, first with the Grameen Bank in Bangladesh and later on a wider, international platform. He is perhaps the ultimate proponent of "capital for good," one of the major trends (if not *the* major trend) to emerge from the flat philanthropic world.

The idea he develops is simple. The market is a unidimensional entity, which exists only for one thing—to make money. We have been very effective at creating markets that have created lots of money, and we have also been very effective at convincing ourselves that what we need and yearn for above all else is money. The problem, Yunus argues, is that human beings are not unidimensional beings. We have feelings, emotions, irrationalities, thoughts, dreams, and so on that make us slightly more complicated than a market. (Which is why people are often perceived by economists as being imperfections in the market!). As a result, it should be possible to offer two markets—one to make money, and another to do good. Companies should be able to choose whether they want to make lots of money or use their activity to do good in the world (the latter accepting that they would probably not make as much money, but might feel better about life as a result).

Capital being used for good. Could this just be the future?

Recently, Ban Ki Moon, the UN secretary general, created a new special envoy post at the organization's headquarters in New York to investigate alternative sources of financing for the Millennium Development Goals. Faced with a cash shortfall of upwards of $50 billion annually to reach the goals by 2015, the former French minister of foreign affairs, Philippe Douste-Blazy, has been tasked with examining how to raise serious amounts of money quickly.

I was lucky enough to be part of a consultation team working with Douste-Blazy and his team in 2008, and the findings from the group were stark. Philanthropy was not going to be an option. In order to get this kind of money together, the kind of money that can bring quantum change, philanthropy was small fry. An altogether different approach was needed, one that would involve freeing up capital to be invested and used for good. For results. For a better world.

From two totally different starting points, Yunus and Douste-Blazy were coming to the same conclusion. Social enterprise, the freeing up of capital for good, and social investment were likely to free up much more positive change than philanthropy in both the short term and the long term.

Is philanthropy failing? Could it be that the philanthropic model is becoming so polluted with short-term individual need that it is losing sight of the big picture and as a result failing to pull together the kind of money needed to promote real change?

How else could we explain the fact that in 1985, the Live Aid concerts around the world asked people to put their hands in their pockets and give money, while in 2005, the Live 8 concerts asked people to put their hands on their keyboards and give their voice as a way to lobby the G-8 leaders to make change that would go way beyond philanthropy? As Bob Geldof said during his keynote speech at the Association of Fundraising Professionals Conference in San Diego in 2008: "In 1985 we raised $200 million. In 2005 we lobbied for change and got $50 billion."

Is philanthropy a stopgap or a solution? If you listen to Yunus and Geldof, it would appear that they are saying it is the former—that it is essential, but that in the flat philanthropic world, in order to meet a set of exponential needs, we need more than philanthropy. We need to:

- Mobilize capital for good.
- Facilitate changes in policy that would produce more equity and reduce the need for philanthropy as a long-term solution.
- Facilitate changes that would make it more attractive to invest capital in the long term for good.

There is still enough money saved in banks, endowments, and investments today to deal with the world's problems—starting of course with the Millennium Development Goals. The problem today, according to Yunus, is that it is being invested in such a way that it is making the wrong people richer and is being driven toward short-term gain. This capital, if invested in long-term projects to help communities develop through integration of social business and enterprise, and accompanied by governmental investments in infrastructure, education, and technology, could have much more positive outputs for the world of tomorrow.

I would argue that philanthropy today is, on the whole, not having this debate. We are not seeing ourselves as a springboard or a conduit for larger, more fundamental change. Unless philanthropy can reposition itself as a facilitator for this *big* change, it will be out-performed and outsmarted by new business and eco-nomically motivated, results-driven social enterprise.

Jeremy Hockenstein is a Harvard graduate who at the end of his studies was faced with the double-whammy choice laid out for us by Yunus: make money or do good. Jeremy did what many of his generation are now doing—decided to not make the choice, but to actively choose both.

He started a not-for-profit firm in Cambodia called Digital Divide to provide outsourced data entry serv-ices for American companies. The company provides, at a reduced rate, data entry services to U.S. companies that most would not be able to afford if done within the United States. At the same time, it pays its Cambodian employees twice the minimum wage for a part-time job, while providing scholarships for its employees to go to school. The company has developed partnerships in Cambodia with educational NPOs working with the poorest of the poor to train new employees, thereby ensuring that kids who might have ended up living off landfill sites now have a future for themselves and their families. One such organization is Digital Bridges (www.passerellesnumeriques.org), a French organization founded by Virginie Legrand—a true visionary who first traveled to Cambodia after more than 15 years spent working in the commercial sector. Upon her return, her desire to help, to make a difference, to bring about real quantum change to kids living in the worst poverty manifested itself through her understanding of the world of capital, and of the fact that capital can be good. Together with Jeremy, they are transforming lives and doing good. Capital for good.

The opportunity for companies is huge. Business models are being reinvented across the world as we speak. Capital for good. NGOs and business. Business making the world a better place. Hewlett-Packard (HP) is one of many companies asking the new $64 million question: "What can we sell to poor people that could improve their lives?" Far from being a mercenary way of exploiting those in poverty, companies big and small have realized that there can be a fit between making money and making a difference—as long we are prepared to think about our economic models differently. HP came up with a solar-powered mobile photo studio that poor Indian women could use to provide affordable photos to their communities, especially important in the bureaucracy of modern India where villagers often have to spend days travelling on buses to cities to get passport-sized photos done for the interminable stream of official papers that the Indian state seems to demand of its citizens. HP found a way to generate income while providing a much-needed service to poor people at an affordable price. The result—HP makes money, the women who run the micro-enterprises doing the photos make money, and the community benefits. This seems to make sense, doesn't it?

So how can we apply this type of thinking to ourselves? Well, if the Kiva adventure has taught us anything, it is that donors would rather invest than give. I mean, who wouldn't? When you have the choice between putting down a sum of money to help a cause and reaching the desired impact once, or putting down the same sum of money and reaching the desired impact a potentially infinite number of times, I know which one I'd choose! Those of us with endowments like to say that we meet this donor need. We are all about investment. The money carries on working, potentially infinitely, through the endowment.

Balancing Out the Future Fundraising Mix

But I'm afraid we've got it all wrong. We are not building long-term replication through an endowment. We are not allowing our donors to achieve the desired impact of their gift before returning their money to them to start over. We are not building capacity in a sustainable way. I believe that we have turned fundraising from a sustainable source of income into an unsustainable source that is a perpetual challenge to mobilize. In pure economic terms, fundraising is horribly inefficient. Every time we need money we need to go and ask. We need to find new people to give to us, or help our existing donors to understand how and why to give us more. We have to grapple with lower and lower retention rates, with increasing competition and the fact that the sustainability model is simply not there. In layman's terms, we have to start more or less at zero each time we start a big campaign. How many successful companies would do that? How many IBMs or Apples would reinvent the wheel each time they put out a new product?

So, we need to build sustainability into the fundraising model. How do we do that? Well, Kiva has shown us one model, but there are many others. In moving from a donation model to an investment model, we all have the opportunity to rebuild our organizations and create systems for our donors where they bring value. Instead of an educational foundation offering one endowed scholarship, why not ask the donor to invest in the students?

Let's say that it costs $500,000 to endow one scholarship at a major U.S. university (at a cost of $25,000 per student per year). This money will finance one student for the length of his or her studies (three to four years). After their term is complete, the scholarship is given to the next student. Over a period of 10 years, the donor will therefore be helping three individuals. But what if the donor gave that $500,000 to the foundation, which then lent it to four students who had the talent but not the financial wherewithal to attend the university. After graduating and finding gainful employment, they would begin to pay back the loan, probably taking 5 to 10 years to do so. As the money comes back in, the donor, through the foundation, can lend it out again, thus renewing the donor's commitment to the university, offering new opportunities for upgrading, and after the same 10-year period ensuring that potentially up to twice as many students have been supported.

But more to the point, the donors will not be feeling that their money has disappeared into a bottomless pit, but that you are using it sensibly, intelligently, and helping them achieve their philanthropic objectives (which, as we know from previous chapters, is going to be one of the major philanthropic drivers tomorrow). You will not be a charity campaigning around a cause and blinded by ideology in your methods, but a smart, twenty-first-century organization working with all the available tools in the flat world to make the most difference to those who matter most—your donors and your beneficiaries.

All not-for-profit organizations add value. Even if the capital impact of this value is not as direct as the scholarship example just given, it does exist. Whether we are helping ex-convicts suffering from drug addictions re-enter society, or homeless people move off the street into sheltered accommodation, or starving children in Africa have food, we are adding value to the world. And this value has a capital impact. The problem is simply that we don't know how to measure it.

The economist and author Joseph Stiglitz argues, oh so rightly, that "we strive for what we can measure." If we don't know how to measure or quantify the value-added impact that our work has on the world, then his thesis is that we won't strive for it. This is a hypothesis that seems to resonate with truth! If we, as charities, are not able to measure it, we cannot put it up there with our unique selling points, and the world will never understand how valuable we are as organizations.

If some of this seems a bit vague and conceptual, I have put together a value-added checklist that works across the board with every type of organization. It is a simple tool to help better understand what you need to be measuring, and once you've measured it, what you then need to be striving for.

1. What do we do?
2. Why is it important and urgent?
3. What is it that we do better than anyone else on the face of the planet?
4. How does this make the world a better place?
5. Precisely who benefits from this work?
6. How do they benefit?
7. How can we quantify (and qualify) this benefit?

Balancing Out the Future Fundraising Mix

By going through the seven stages of the value-added checklist, you will be a step closer to working out how to move from a write-off model to an investment model. By quantifying just what value our organizations bring to the world, and who benefits from it, we are suddenly catapulted into the arena of investment, of credibility, and of state-of-the-art management.

But this is where we come back to individuals. At a fundamental level, the work that companies like HP are doing in developing countries does seem to echo the fact that some of them have started to look differently at their business models (as we should be doing, too!) and integrate some notion of capital and good. Others will inevitably follow.

Is the fact that it is all about sales necessarily a bad thing? No, because companies are not fundamentally philanthropic. And they shouldn't be. But let's trace the idea of capital for good back awhile. Where did it originate? What was the aha moment that made big corporate-ville sit up and smell the fair trade coffee? Quite simply, it was . . . us! The Western consumer. The "demanding dictator" cited by Kjell Nordstrom and Jonas Ridderstrale. The change in values over the past decade in most Western countries has not been just an evolution, but a true sea change. Let's return to that recent study carried out in France which showed that 82 percent of all consumers would rather purchase a product—given equal pricing and quality—from a *socially responsible company.* In order to access this market, the vast majority of companies will be happy paying lip service to corporate social responsibility, just doing enough so that they can put some stuff on their web site and write a nice few pages in their annual reports.

But some, like HP and a number of others, have taken things one stage further—not in the linear way that perhaps many observers might have expected, but in a *global citizenship* way. This consumer values revolution was a fundamental mover in helping companies start to consider themselves members of the global community. And in doing so, it has changed the paradigm. We are not just about doing things more *responsibly*; we are now about rethinking our whole economic model and wondering what tomorrow will be made of. Horizons have been broadened. And at the basis of this are individuals—people like you and me, who broadened their own horizons and forced companies and big business to follow suit. Now, as often happens in the world of capital, the latter are starting to overtake the former as they see market and growth opportunities. It remains therefore the role of the individual to keep things on an even keel, to keep horizons where they should be, and to keep the focus, as much as possible, on the value of innovation to the world as a whole.

We are living in powerful times. These are times of revolution—well-managed, digitalized and talent-led revolution, but revolution nonetheless.

We are opening our minds to the realities that people, wherever they are in the world, are connected in ways we could not have imagined just a decade ago. Every human being wishes the same things for their children—to work hard and ensure a better life for the next generation. Whether we are in Cardiff, Calgary, California, or Calcutta, we share this fundamental truth. Yet, for years, we have built organizations to provide help and assistance, rather than listening to what those we are trying to help have to say to us. Who knows better what you need in order to provide a better life for your children than you? Together, we are moving to a world where we stop providing answers for people who already have answers and we start asking the right questions and listening to the answers we are given. As Muhammad Yunus says so wonderfully, a bonsai is grown from the seed of a giant redwood, taken from the forest and put into a tiny restricted pot. The flat philanthropic world is our chance to take the tiny pots that we have put ourselves, our beneficiaries, and billions of other people into, and open them up to the forest—so that the bonsai trees become redwoods.

My experience of individuals in poverty is that they are the most determined people in the world. Our job is to find ways to free them from the bonds that are holding them back. And today we have the tools to do this, in ways that would not have been imaginable just ten or even five years ago. From social networking, to peer-to-peer giving, to new economic models, to capital for good . . . we have opportunities like we have never before imagined. Our time is now. And with that comes responsibility. We have the chance to make the world a better place. We have the tools to do it. The money is there. It is now up to us. We no longer have a choice. For dozens of years, the third sector has been a hotbed of mediocrity. We have been all about the touchy-feely things, about making people feel good, and about staying as far away as possible from the hard and uncomfortable decisions that could make a real difference but mean embracing difficult change. Today, we no longer have this luxury. The world knows. It knows that we have the opportunity and the tools to change it. It is watching us. And it is generally not impressed.

Conclusion

We have a huge responsibility today, and we will have even more tomorrow. Our beneficiaries are depending on us. As an Australian fundraiser friend said to me recently (with typical Aussie tact), "If your charity exists to save lives, and you are not doing your utmost, every day, to raise the most money—even if that means taking some really hard and uncomfortable decisions—then people are dying as a result of your mediocrity, which is tantamount to manslaughter."

Ten years ago we could get away with it. Today, the world knows better. And we should too. Welcome to the flat philanthropic world. Go out there, grab it, and shake it down. Let's dream the world of tomorrow. And make it happen.

Acknowledgments

As any author will testify, writing a first book is a most traumatic experience. You are putting your thoughts, work, and ideas out to the world with no idea of what will happen next. Jumping over this threshold has been made possible for me only through the support and patience of so many people that the list would be frankly embarrassing. But I trust you know who you are. I would, however, like to extend a special thank-you to a couple of friends and colleagues whose input into these pages has been essential and whose advice and guidance have been second to none.

Deb Ward and Noémie Wiroth for being part of the idea that led to this book in the first place. Aimee Priscaro, on whose deck and kitchen table a large chunk of it was written. Kay Sprinkel Grace, Tony Myers, Tony Elischer, Sonya Swiridjuk and Ilana

Landsberg-Lewis for their inspiration and for showing me what to aim for. Daryl Upsall and Balazs Sator for giving up their time to share their stories. Andrew Watt for being the other half of globalization and philanthropy. And Mum, Dad, Anna, and Hélène for putting up with me.

And a final thank-you to everyone who shares the passion of potential and who loves the joy of sharing the gentle art of giving.

AFP Code of Ethical Principles and Standards

ETHICAL PRINCIPLES • Adopted 1964; amended Sept. 2007

The Association of Fundraising Professionals (AFP) exists to foster the development and growth of fundraising professionals and the profession, to promote high ethical behavior in the fundraising profession and to preserve and enhance philanthropy and volunteerism. Members of AFP are motivated by an inner drive to improve the quality of life through the causes they serve. They serve the ideal of philanthropy, are committed to the preservation and enhancement of volunteerism; and hold stewardship of these concepts as the overriding direction of their professional life. They recognize their responsibility to ensure that needed resources are vigorously and ethically sought and that the intent of the donor is honestly fulfilled. To these ends, AFP members, both individual and business, embrace certain values that they strive to uphold in performing their responsibilities for generating philanthropic support. AFP business members strive to promote and protect the work and mission of their client organizations.

AFP members both individual and business aspire to:

- practice their profession with integrity, honesty, truthfulness and adherence to the absolute obligation to safeguard the public trust
- act according to the highest goals and visions of their organizations, professions, clients and consciences
- put philanthropic mission above personal gain;
- inspire others through their own sense of dedication and high purpose
- improve their professional knowledge and skills, so that their performance will better serve others
- demonstrate concern for the interests and well-being of individuals affected by their actions
- value the privacy, freedom of choice and interests of all those affected by their actions
- foster cultural diversity and pluralistic values and treat all people with dignity and respect
- affirm, through personal giving, a commitment to philanthropy and its role in society
- adhere to the spirit as well as the letter of all applicable laws and regulations
- advocate within their organizations adherence to all applicable laws and regulations
- avoid even the appearance of any criminal offense or professional misconduct
- bring credit to the fundraising profession by their public demeanor
- encourage colleagues to embrace and practice these ethical principles and standards
- be aware of the codes of ethics promulgated by other professional organizations that serve philanthropy

ETHICAL STANDARDS

Furthermore, while striving to act according to the above values, AFP members, both individual and business, agree to abide (and to ensure, to the best of their ability, that all members of their staff abide) by the AFP standards. Violation of the standards may subject the member to disciplinary sanctions, including expulsion, as provided in the AFP Ethics Enforcement Procedures.

MEMBER OBLIGATIONS

1. Members shall not engage in activities that harm the members' organizations, clients or profession.
2. Members shall not engage in activities that conflict with their fiduciary, ethical and legal obligations to their organizations, clients or profession.
3. Members shall effectively disclose all potential and actual conflicts of interest; such disclosure does not preclude or imply ethical impropriety.
4. Members shall not exploit any relationship with a donor, prospect, volunteer, client or employee for the benefit of the members or the members' organizations.
5. Members shall comply with all applicable local, state, provincial and federal civil and criminal laws.
6. Members recognize their individual boundaries of competence and are forthcoming and truthful about their professional experience and qualifications and will represent their achievements accurately and without exaggeration.
7. Members shall present and supply products and/or services honestly and without misrepresentation and will clearly identify the details of those products, such as availability of the products and/or services and other factors that may affect the suitability of the products and/or services for donors, clients or nonprofit organizations.
8. Members shall establish the nature and purpose of any contractual relationship at the outset and will be responsive and available to organizations and their employing organizations before, during and after any sale of materials and/or services. Members will comply with all fair and reasonable obligations created by the contract.

9. Members shall refrain from knowingly infringing the intellectual property rights of other parties at all times. Members shall address and rectify any inadvertent infringement that may occur.
10. Members shall protect the confidentiality of all privileged information relating to the provider/client relationships.
11. Members shall refrain from any activity designed to disparage competitors untruthfully.

SOLICITATION AND USE OF PHILANTHROPIC FUNDS

12. Members shall take care to ensure that all solicitation and communication materials are accurate and correctly reflect their organizations' mission and use of solicited funds.
13. Members shall take care to ensure that donors receive informed, accurate and ethical advice about the value and tax implications of contributions.
14. Members shall take care to ensure that contributions are used in accordance with donors' intentions.
15. Members shall take care to ensure proper stewardship of all revenue sources, including timely reports on the use and management of such funds.
16. Members shall obtain explicit consent by donors before altering the conditions of financial transactions.

PRESENTATION OF INFORMATION

17. Members shall not disclose privileged or confidential information to unauthorized parties.
18. Members shall adhere to the principle that all donor and prospect information created by, or on behalf of, an organization or a client is the property of that organization or client and shall not be transferred or utilized except on behalf of that organization or client.
19. Members shall give donors and clients the opportunity to have their names removed from lists that are sold to, rented to or exchanged with other organizations.
20. Members shall, when stating fundraising results, use accurate and consistent accounting methods that conform to the appropriate guidelines adopted by the American Institute of Certified Public Accountants (AICPA)* for the type of organization involved. (* In countries outside of the United States, comparable authority should be utilized.)

COMPENSATION AND CONTRACTS

21. Members shall not accept compensation or enter into a contract that is based on a percentage of contributions; nor shall members accept finder's fees or contingent fees. Business members must refrain from receiving compensation from third parties derived from products or services for a client without disclosing that third-party compensation to the client (for example, volume rebates from vendors to business members).
22. Members may accept performance-based compensation, such as bonuses, provided such bonuses are in accord with prevailing practices within the members' own organizations and are not based on a percentage of contributions.
23. Members shall neither offer nor accept payments or special considerations for the purpose of influencing the selection of products or services.
24. Members shall not pay finder's fees, commission or percentage compensation based on contributions, and shall take care to discourage their organizations from making such payments.
25. Any member receiving funds on behalf of a donor or client must meet the legal requirements for the disbursement of those funds. Any interest or income earned on the funds should be fully disclosed.

207

A Donor Bill of Rights

PHILANTHROPY is based on voluntary action for the common good. It is a tradition of giving and sharing that is primary to the quality of life. To assure that philanthropy merits the respect and trust of the general public, and that donors and prospective donors can have full confidence in the not-for-profit organizations and causes they are asked to support, we declare that all donors have these rights:

I.

To be informed of the organization's mission, of the way the organization intends to use donated resources, and of its capacity to use donations effectively for their intended purposes.

II.

To be informed of the identity of those serving on the organization's governing board, and to expect the board to exercise prudent judgement in its stewardship responsibilities.

III.

To have access to the organization's most recent financial statements.

IV.

To be assured their gifts will be used for the purposes for which they were given.

V.

To receive appropriate acknowledgement and recognition.

VI.

To be assured that information about their donations is handled with respect and with confidentiality to the extent provided by law.

VII.

To expect that all relationships with individuals representing organizations of interest to the donor will be professional in nature.

VIII.

To be informed whether those seeking donations are volunteers, employees of the organization or hired solicitors.

IX.

To have the opportunity for their names to be deleted from mailing lists that an organization may intend to share.

X.

To feel free to ask questions when making a donation and to receive prompt, truthful and forthright answers.

DEVELOPED BY
Association for Healthcare Philanthropy (AHP)
Association of Fundraising Professionals (AFP)
Council for Advancement and Support of Education (CASE)
Giving Institute: Leading Consultants to Non-Profits

ENDORSED BY
(in formation)
Independent Sector
National Catholic Development Conference (NCDC)
National Committee on Planned Giving (NCPG)
Council for Resource Development (CRD)
United Way of America

About the Author

Jon Duschinsky is the founder of bethechange Consulting, an international network of fundraising and communication consultants for the nonprofit sector.

A founding member of the fundraising group Cascaid in the United Kingdom, and a leading actor on the European fundraising stage, Jon has been a board member of the European Fundraising Association and both the chair and director of the French Institute of Fundraising. He now works hands-on advising nongovernmental organizations (NGOs), universities, schools, cultural organizations, and research centers around the world—creating and delivering made-to-measure capacity-building programs of training and consultancy. He is a recognized speaker at high-profile international events and at universities in Europe and the United States, where he delivers training on inspiration, motivation, and creativity in fundraising practice and theory.

Contact Jon by e-mail: jon@bethechange.fr

Index

Index

Index

Index